Thoroughbreds of Railroading

Yesterday and Today

LOOK AHEAD-LOOK SOUTH

NS Norfolk Southern

A Pictorial Album of Memphis to Chattanooga Area

including

Memphis & Charleston Railroad

Southern Railway System

Norfolk Southern Corporation

Edited by

Jack Daniel

Grandmother Earth Creations
Memphis, Tennessee

Editor
  Jack Daniel
    3467 Alfred Drive
    Memphis, TN 38133
    (901)-386-3604

Publisher:
  Grandmother
  Earth Creations
    P. O. Box 241986
    Memphis, TN 38124

Typography and layout
by Jack Daniel

NS Classifying Yard-Sheffield, AL

LIBRARY OF CONGRESS CARD NUMBER: 99-071728

ISBN 1-884289-26-6

First Printing, 1999

ACKNOWLEDGEMENTS

I would like to extend heartfelt thanks to several people who have contributed to making this book a reality. Production of this book could not have been accomplished without the assiistance of Jimmy W. Edwards, Herbert Meadows, Maynard Kimbrough, B. W. Wells, Aubrey Smith, Melvyn Myhan, Mike D. Warhurst, P. D. Wright, Tim Wagnon, Dave Jordan, Rayburn Pace, Lance Underwood, Bobby Balentine, Jimmy Askew, Bill Hutton, and Mike Q. Malone from the Muscle Shoals Area of Alabama and Barry Boothe and R. K. Thorne from the Iuka, Mississippi area and Clyde Berry from the Knoxville, TN area. All these people deserve our sincerest appreciation.

Front Cover Photograph: Norfolk Southern freight train headed up by locomotive 7037, a GP50, leads an eastbound (probably train # 390) out of a fog at Wilmuth Street overpass in Iuka, MS at 7:36 a.m. June 3, 1996. Photo by Barry Boothe in Jack Daniel Collection.

TABLE OF CONTENTS

Chapter One   Introduction ....Page   1

Chapter Two   Yesterday's Railroad Men & Machines......... Page   7

Chapter Three   Yesterday's Railroad Forms........................ Page   93

Chapter Four   Today's Railroad Men & Machines.............. Page   105

Chapter Five   Today's Railroad Forms............................. Page   267

Appendix   N. S. Seniority Lists..................................... Page   275

Index   Names of people who are photographed ... Page   304

Hands upon the throttle and eyes upon the rail. Photo by J. J. Young in collection of Jack Daniel.

The New Norfolk Southern System

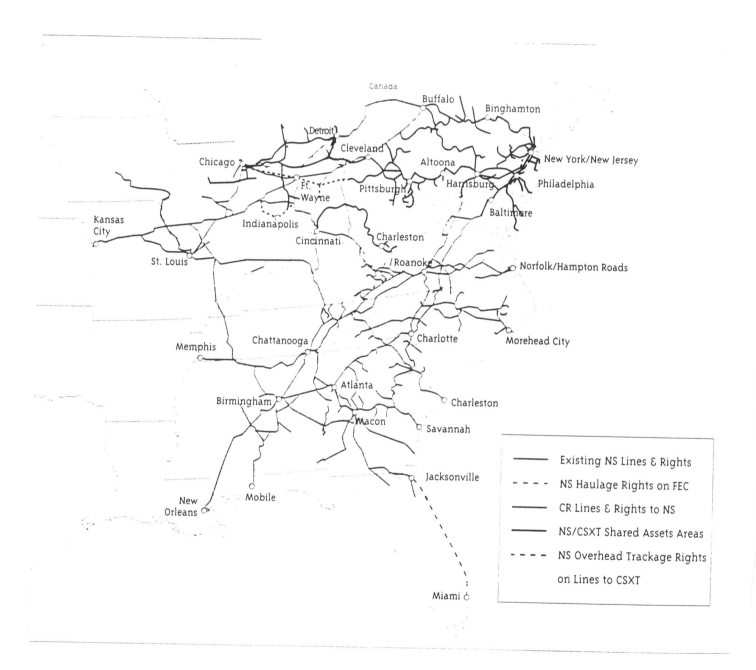

———	Existing NS Lines & Rights
- - - -	NS Haulage Rights on FEC
———	CR Lines & Rights to NS
———	NS/CSXT Shared Assets Areas
- - - -	NS Overhead Trackage Rights on Lines to CSXT

Chapter One

INTRODUCTION

On June 1, 1982, the day Southern Railway joined Norfolk & Western Railway to form the Norfolk Southern Corporation, engineers from each railroad shake hands as a symbol of the new partnership.

See back of book for index of people whose pictures are in this album.

INTRODUCTION

This pictorial story is presented to depict locomotives and the railroad people who kept the trains running in the earlier days and continue to do so today. Photographs selected for Chapter 2 generally depict pioneers of the steam era that helped shape railroad history, generally pre-1950, and a few from the turn of the century, in the area between Memphis and Chattanooga, Tennessee. Chapter 4 is of the diesel era and the people necessary to run the railroad in more modern times up to the present.

Railroad men often look to statistics, such as "gross ton-miles per train hour," to measure accomplishments. Just as a matter of information, the September, 1997, issue of TRAINS Magazine tells us that the world's heaviest train was run in Australia. The mega-train consisted of 10 diesel locomotives, distributed throughout the train, and 540 loaded cars with 62,263 tons of ore. The Train, over 3 and 1/2 miles long, was operated to ensure that the DPU (distributed power units) were capable of performing to specification. There are no plans to run regular trains of this length.

Those original FTs and early E6s, Alco FAs and DL109 diesels swept steam locomotives aside. Then came the EMDs GP9, Alco RS11, ugly "road switcher" things that could go anywhere and do anything. There was a grudging realization that the GP9 was a machine to be respected. You could pick up and drop cars, go down long hills with dynamic brakes singing, listen to them talk it up going up hills with tonnage, enjoy the ride of the good old leaf-sprung Blomberg trucks at 60-plus miles per hour on time freights and 75 m.p.h. on passenger trains. As for its looks, it was a far cry from the steam locomotives we had grown up with and loved.

But progress could not be held back. The Electro Motive Division of General Motors soon came out with more powerful EMD locomotives equipped with turbochargers and six traction motors, and immediately it seemed that dependability started a downward slide. There were more sophisticated things for controlling wheel slip which occurred more now in trying to harness the horsepower of the turbocharged engines. Transition program switches and shunt resistors failed. A new phrase called "acceptable failure rates" came into mechanical department vocabulary. The frequency of the failures might not have been high, but when you were the guy trying to get the piggyback over the road on time, or were on the side of a hill with what was called "jam-up" tonnage, any failure was not good.

But the GP9 kept rolling along. It took a lot of them to put enough horsepower on the drawbar of a long piggyback train to run 60 m. p. h., but you knew that when you reduced the throttle the engine would not choke to death because a turbocharger did not come back on the gear train that drove it at low r.p.m.s, or that a program switch would not malfunction or a shunt resistor open and rob you of a unit's worth of power during acceleration. Turbocharged power became much more dependable and the development of alternators for traction power helped immensely.

Taking a look at SD-40 and SD-45s, some engineers have said if they break down we can fix them. If one fails on a hill, a savvy conductor can get it running again and keep us moving. If we do stall and get the unit running, an SD-40 or SD-45 will dig in and restart a heavy train better than any other locomotive. They are powerful enough to pull your back teeth out, and they are quiet, but they are not without quirks. There is not much leg room and the controls just don't seem right. They wonder how using a computer to perform a simple task such as cutting out the air brakes can be called an improvement. They don't much like having a computer, an electriic motor, and electric wires, all of which can fail, between them and their air brakes. The simple valve on the old air systems seemed to work fine.

Some engineers have said they never thought they could miss an SD-40-2, as ubiquitous as they have been. But when it comes time to running a creeping coal train all night, those old workhorses are like a pair of comfortable house slippers when waiting for hours for a green signal or a track gang or a yardmaster. The whisper cabs are quiet, but in an old unit your knees aren't always knocking the console. And there is something to be said for those individual heaters too.

When remote control power was introduced 30 years ago, the equipment was so big it filled an entire baggage car. Today the computer, called the Locotrol system, can fit inside the nose of the engine and is light enough for a person to carry. Remote control helper equipment that Union Pacific Railroad calls DPU or Distributed Power Units, "slave units" placed at rear of trains and controlled from the head end has helped overcome past problems. The GE Harris Company contends its system will create more control for the engineer thus reducing slack action. Faster acceleration and shorter stopping distances will improve train scheduling. Increased speed in charging brake pipes means reduced delays. U. P. believes slack will be reduced 50 per cent on heavy trains.

With (P.T.S.) Positive Train Separation and (P.T.C.) Positive Train Control, and combing the next-generation electronic air brake with LocoControl are projects in the making. Trains will be able to run closer together because the dispatcher will know where they are by global positioning satellite information and other data transmitted from the on-board computer. This information will help prevent trains from colliding when the engineer does not respond. It isn't if PTC is something new. It's just a new name for what we once called automatic train control. When the federal regulatory commissions realized that the testing of the newer technology was for merely validating software, they are faced with a growing public awareness of more freight trains in their back yards, and they are becoming upset with railroads, and demanding that the FRA do something about chemical-fed fires from derailments, especially when one happens in a heavily populated area. So we can expect increased attention to the subject of safety on the railroads. Increased attention must also be focused on the matter of human fatigue of train crews and the possibility that employees will be subjected to harassment to keep the trains moving.

Because of the uncommon hours that some train crews work and the possibility that they turn up to work with less than a complete sleep quota, then it is obvious that at some time during a shift they will feel tired and start to nod off. Some railroads are borrowing ideas from NASA to implement sleep management techniques. Napping is just one aspect of current efforts aimed at developing

4

fatigue countermeasures. Napping would be permitted only under certain conditions and only on stopped trains, such as those waiting in a siding for track work, or other situations. One crew member must remain awake at all times. Napping will not be allowed to interfere with or delay the movement of traffic. Booklets have been prepared to show how to cope with working shifts and foods to eat before, during and after a shift, that will enable sleep to be gained easier at the completion of the work period.

Still at it in 1998, after vanquishing steam with teams of F units, EMD unveils its latest, the SD90MAC, powered by a new four-cycle diesel, the 6,000 h.p. H-engine. The "90Mac" is big and weighs 425,000 pounds and is 80 feet long. The "90Mac's" 6,000 horsepower for tractions equals 1,000 usable horsepower per axle. Now this lets us admire modern things but we are sweeping some old stuff under the rug. In 1914, we had hand-fired steam engines that had 1,125 usable drawbar horsepower per axle. So here we are, 83 years later, trumpeting about a locomotive which has achieved 1,000 horsepower per axle. Jacking up the horsepower of the prime mover and making a machine that could turn it into usable power was not easy. Adhesion was always supposed to have been the diesel's strong point. Advertising for the diesel made its adhesion a great selling point over steam. EMD representatives bragged about the adhesion in the 18-20 percent range. Steam locomotives had always been figured capable of around 25 percent adhesion. It's amazing how long it has taken to reach 1,000 usable horsepower per axle. Even with 83 years of technological progress, they still haven't beat the steam locomotive. 1

Norfolk Southern Corporation was formed June 1, 1982, with the consolidation of Norfolk & Western Railway and the Southern Railway System. Both companies brought into the union a reputation for sound, sensible management and a tradition of quality and reliability. Since then, Norfolk Southern has continued and built upon that reputation, identifying new markets, adapting to ever-changing market conditions, innovating new services and technologies and growing steadily year after year.

In addition to the railroad, Norfolk Southern formerly owned North American Van Lines but sold this subsidiary on January 12, 1998 to Clayton, Dubilier & Rice Inc. Another subsidiary that is owned by Norfolk Southern Corporation is the Pocahontas Land Corporation which manages approximately 900,000 acres of coal, natural gas and timber resources in Alabama, Illinois, Kentucky, Tennessee, Virginia and West Virginia. 2

CSX and Norfolk Southern on June 23, 1997, weighed in with an 8 volume, 14,810-page, 74-pound argument telling the federal regulators why a carved up Conrail is better than an independent Conrail, and details a litany of service improvements such as: shorter transit times - new single-line service for over 233,000 shipments a year of autos, chemicals, agricultural items and other general merchandise. This plan was approved and implementation should be completed sometime in 1999. There will be a third region added but the eastern and western regions will remain basically the same. The new northern region will have the Harrisburg, Pittsburgh and Dearborn divisions. The eastern region still has the Georgia, Piedmont, Pocahontas and Virginia divisions and our western region will still have the Alabama, Illinois, Kentucky, Lake and Tennessee divisions.3

The railroad between Memphis and Chattanooga occupies a strategic geographical region in the South. It provides a gateway to the Southwest for goods coming from the East and vice versa. The ardent builders and promoters of this road did not give up. They persevered through many extreme difficulties. At the time this road was built there was a Land-Grant law on record but this road was built without any government aid of any kind. The only government favors it received was after the Civil War when it was allowed to purchase locomotives and railroad material from the U. S. Government on credit.

Norfolk Southern Railroad, like most other roads, has present day railroaders who are descendents from a long line of railroaders. Why would so many people continue, generation after generation, if railroading was not enjoyable and fun? Some say it is enjoyable; others deny it and go on to call railroad work the most backbreaking, grueling, miserable experience of their lives. There is a tendency for people to overlook this very important aspect of railroad work: It was and is fun. Perhaps not every job nor every day was fun but you have to take the bad with the good. But for a lot of folks, working on the railroad was - and is still - challenging, varied, and enjoyable. It could - and can - be better than factory work or operating a farm tractor, and there was - and is - always a chance of promotion. I have heard it said that as we get older we become more and more the stuff our forebears put into us.

Most all railroaders enjoy working with other railroaders. You are all there to do a job, and getting through one more day is a real accomplishment. Retired railroaders gather regularly over coffee all across the country to talk about the good times, laugh about embarrassing situations, and agonize over the problems. Throughout, there is the camaraderie, the good fellowship, and the opportunity to relax, knowing they can look back on "a job well done." That camaraderie will hopefully continue for future generations. But some families lost members to railroad accidents. The "safety first" movement, going back to 1910, has been another part of the tradition for many years. Safety is the top priority for most railroaders. Railroaders should - and can - be proud of their work. Through their efforts, the area between Memphis and Chattanooga and between Sheffield and Birmingham has enjoyed economic growth and expansion and much gainful employment.

"Railroading does get in your blood," as the old saying goes. That is desirable because it has provided many good and dedicated railroaders. People are the driving force of history. It is my desire that this book, that combines yesterday with today, will become a useful tool for looking at the local history of railroading for generations to come. Perhaps this book will help keep the memory alive of those railroaders who have passed on. Hopefully it will encourage future railroaders to continue the practice of recording railroad history and remembering their fellow workers.

So now, let us begin our exploration of the railroad linking Memphis with Chattanooga, Tennessee, and observe this pictorial history from the perspective of those who actually lived it and are living it today. These echoes from the past will, I hope, complement the current photographs to make our journey through the years more intimately meaningful.

6

I want to know I've left behind
Some "good" before I'm gone.
I hope that in my latter years
In all honesty I can say:
That somewhere in my lifetime,
I have brightened a railroader's day.
That maybe I have brought a smile
To some engineer's face.
And made one moment a little nicer
While they railroaded in this place.
For if not a heart be touched by me,
And not a smile was left behind,
Then this book that I edited
Could have been a waste of time.
With all my heart, I truly hope
To leave something here on earth...
That touched someone, made him smile
And contributed to my life, Worth.

The Editor

I truly would have liked to have had <u>color</u> pictures in this book but the cost would have been prohibitive. I would have had to charge from $60 to $70 per copy and I realized that would prevent many people from purchasing the book.

Chapter Two

Yesterday's Railroad

Men & Machines

There was an incredible effort needed to keep the engines of American commerce moving. There were heroes who did their jobs with professionalism and pride, ensuring prompt delivery of goods and safety of crews and passengers. They remind us of the time before the computer, before robotic assembly lines, before microwave radios and enclosed cabs, when the story was of *men and machines*.

The Old Iron Horse

As our thoughts often wander, back to things we love so well,
We think of the "Old Iron Horse" that once proudly rode the rails.
It was the pride of all railroads, an engineers dream.
I can still see her drivers rolling and hear the whistle scream.
Hear the main rod pounding, see the firebox gleam.
It was a thrill for every engineer, to run an engine driven by steam.
When she headed in a siding, people would gather all around ,
To hear the firebox roaring, see the steam gauge on two hundred pounds.
It was fascinating to the young, thrilling to the old,
To watch the skilled fireman, as he shoveled on the coal.
Could see the steam gauge climbing, getting ready to make up time.
See the smoke stack rolling, getting ready the grade to climb.
The engineer checking the water glass, also watching the rail,
He will make the schedule before him, he will do it without fail.
We never want to hold back progress, so diesels shoved aside our steam.
All we have left of the "Old Iron Horse" are memories and bygone dreams.
Diesels are not near as fascinating, as the days we had our steam.
So until something is more thrilling, we will hold to our memories of steam.

Maynard Kimbrough

Written in 1975
Maynard Kimbrough
Retired Southern Railway Engineer

Corinth, MS town square with union pickets on duty behind cotton bales after the battle of Corinth. A hotel, restaurant, grocery, and saloon line streets where Union troops ran for their lives in front of a Rebel charge Octiber 4, 1862. Xerox copy in editor's files.

A Memphis & Charleston Railroad train at Corinth, MS in 1862. The 2 story Tishomingo Hotel and the M&C depot are on left of tracks. 135 years later, one Norfolk Southern train can carry more freight tonnage on one trip than the Memphis & Charleston Railroad would carry in a year. Xerox copy in editor's file.

Huntsville, AL was considered the watercress capitol of the world at one time. Shown here, east of the depot, in the 1930s are barrels of watercress awaiting shipment. The depot was headquarters for the Memphis & Charleston Railroad from about 1850 until Southern Railway took over in 1894. This building was captured by the Federal Army during the Civil War. Huntsville citizens were successful in getting this building placed on the Register of Historical Buildings. Photo is in Heritage Room of the Huntsville-Madison County Library.

Loading watermellons from a mule-drawn wagon into a wooden boxcar that was felt-lined with hay on the floor. Photo from Southern Railway TIES Magazine. Used with permission

Engine 1721 on Fifth Street in Tuscumbia, AL. Before the bygone era of the steam engine, Southern Railway's locomotive 1721 stopped along Fifth Street in Tuscumbia. This is a scene looking west. From left to right; Ed Hamlet, engineer - Arthur Jackson, fireman - Will Mitchell, foreman - Noah Underwood, switchman - and J. O. Shelly. Photo was furnished by Floyd McCorkle.

A "First" in Sheffield, AL. The first accident in Sheffield involving a train and automobile happened on January 16, 1913, at Raleigh and First Avenue. According to witnesses, W. H. Martin of Sheffield, was driving his car south across the tracks when a line of hopper cars were switched from the westbound engine. The uncoupled cars rolled about 30 feet before striking the auto then dragging the car and driver 60 to 80 feet. Mr. Martin was injured in the accident. Area citizens and railroad personnel witnessing the accident and signing depositions were: R. B. LeMay, Walter Westbrook, R. L. Finchum, Jackson A. Cothren, Luther Martin, C. T. Williams, Abe Goldstein, J. N. Shea, Andrew Watkins and Clyde Harrison. Taken from article in the Colbert County Reporter.

12

Pictured here are Tom Naves (left), conductor and J. W. "Buddy" Edwards, Sr. (right), engineer on Southern Railway 4-4-0 locomotive 2504, on the Riverton, AL Branch. The Riverton Branch was built by the Birmingham, Sheffield & Tennessee River Railroad which later became The Northern Alabama Railroad and finally absorbed into the Southern. This railroad ran from Birmingham to Sheffield, then west to Margerum, AL, then branched off the main line to Riverton, AL where a new town was being built. Photo provided by Jimmy Edwards, Jr. of Sheffield, AL, son of above pictured engineer. Jimmy is a retired Southern Railway engin

1913 photo of Southern Railway 4-4-0 locomotive 2504 at Riverton, AL Branch water tank. Standing by his dog is engineer, J. W. Edwards, Sr. J. W. Edwards, Jr. and Lena Rebecca Edwards were the engineer's children and they hace their caps on. This train usually ran a couple of round-trips from Riverton to the main line at Margerum. Picture provided by Jimmy Edwards, Jr., retired Southern Railway engineer and the boy pictured on front of engine.

Pictured here in this May, 1915 photo of Southern Railway 1014, left to right, is H. W. Ashley, trainmaster, Robert Crawford, fireman who entered service Nov. 2, 1904, and R. J. Wilson, engineer who entered service of the Memphis & Charleston Railroad in March, 1879 and since May of 1887 was assigned to passenger runs. He had only two firemen in thirty-one years. Richard Harris served with him for 16 years and Robert Crawford for 15 years.

Mr. R. J. Wilson had two sons who were engineers. Lewis J. Wilson entered service at the Sheffield Shops as an apprentice mechanic at the age of 17, and he was made a fireman in October , 1910 and promoted to engineer May 22, 1914. W. F. Wilson entered service as a fireman at the age of 15 on June 22, 1911, and was promoted to engineer on October 11, 1914.

Note that the engine was decorated with an American flag draped around the cab window. Attached to the tender is a placard with the words "DAM MUSCLE SHOALS AND DAM IT NOW." That was a time when the citizens of the Tennessee Valley were beginning a campaign to encourage the Federal Government to build a dam on the Tennessee River at Muscle Shoals, AL. Leading business men and politicans of the area had made arrangements for Southern Railway to run a special train from Chattanooga, TN to Sheffield, AL to gather people for a rally to drum up support for the building of the dam.

The photto above is of Second No. 26 for the return trip to Chattanooga. As is the case with any piece of mechanical equipment, breakdowns can be expected. Such was the case with the 1014 as it experienced problems at Leighton, AL and the engine had to be replaced. Since Leighton was only a few miles from Sheffield, the delay was not too long. Engineer Wilson and fireman Crawford prepared for some fast running in order to make up time. It was said that they were only about 10 minutes late in arriving at Chattanooga.

500 M. W.

Form 813

SOUTHERN RAILWAY COMPANY

OFFICE OF

Loyall ala May 12th 1915

Mr R J Wilson Engineer Tuscumbia ala
    Dear Mr Wilson.

I wish   to thank you and your Fireman Robert Crawford for the
excellent run you gave us on 2nd 25 from Chattanooga to Sheffield
sunday   night and for the good run going back on 2nd 26. there

was at no time any   rough handling of the brakes and no
black smoke to   worry the passengers and while we had   the
misfotrune to   have to give up the lo14 at Leighton this was
something   that could not be avoided and had no refellection
  whatever on you or your fireman. everybody was satisfied
and the train only reached Chattanooga ten minutes late for the
passengers to get off and this was   alright and   I was   told by
several ·   that the trip was a sucess in every way.

I thank you both very kindly for the interest in the
matter and hope to be able to call on you many more times to
help me out in the same manner.

Yours Very Truly

H W Ashley

Train Master

Here is a copy of a letter written by trainmaster H. W. Ashley to Mr. R. J. Wilson, engineer, of Loyall, AL. Loyall was the name of the yard that was located west of Montgomery Avenue in Sheffield and ran parallel to Shop Pike. This letter was typical of what priorities a trainmaster had for passenger engineers in that day. It was a nice commendation and one that Mr. Wilson treasured as it was saved in the family scrapbook. Original copy in collection of Jack Daniel, editor,

Pictured standing in front of Memphis & Charleston locomotive # 80, is believed to be at least two members of the crew that was working during the Civil War. On left, the conductor, on right, the engineer. The brakeman is in the middle and the fireman standing above the brakeman. Note that all men are wearing different type caps. If you look closely you can see on the right sleeve of the brakeman is stenciled with the letters M&C. The conductor and engineer were probably working during the 1860s and nearing retirement when this photo was taken in the 1880s. Photo courtesy of Hoole Special Collection Library, The University of Alabama, Tuscakoosa, AL.

A Memphis & Charleston Railroad train crossing Florence Bridge in late 1800s. Photo courtesy Alabama Dept. of Archives and History.

This 1880's photograph of the Memphis & Charleston Railroad office and depot at Memphis shows the building much as it was in 1861. The brick office building (center) was completed in 1859; the freight shed and passenger depot (foreground) in 1860. In editors collection.

This is a photo of Huntsville, Alabama citizens gathered around to see their first diesel locomotive on "The Joe Wheeler" on its inaugural trip in the mid 1930's. Photo in Jack Daniel Collection.

18

This photo is believed to have been made in front of the Forrest Yard office that was built by the Memphis & Charleston Railroad. Some special event drew these employees and their families to the office. The photographer must have failed to tell them to "smile" as this is a rather somber looking group. This is the right side of a large photo and the left side will follow on next page. Photo courtesy of Shirley Stewart Perry whose grandfather, W. A. Stewart, was a Southern Railway section foreman and who retired in 1949.

This photo was made in front of what is believed to be the Forrest Yard Office built by the Memphis & Charleston Railroad. Some special event must have drawn these rather somber looking employees and their families together. This is the right half of a large photo. The left half is on the preceeding page. Photo courtesy of Shirley Stewart Perry whose grandfather, W. A. Stewart, was a section foreman and who retired in 1949.

20

Memphis & Charleston locomotive # 201 at Decatur, AL in 1887. Engineer E. H. Clem is third from left. It is doubtful that these clothes would have been worn on a workday. Note the engine has no pilot or cowcatcher so it could have been in yard service. Photo in Jack Daniel Collection.

No, this is not the aftermath of a tornado. This is the old Forrest Yard office building being torn down around 1982. This was the second yard office building and the present day tower is the third. Photo by John Rea, in Jack Daniel Collection.

Southern Railway engineer Jimmy W. Edwards (promoted 10-12-42) of Sheffield, AL on locomotive # 77 on a steam powered excursion from Sheffield to Huntsville and return in 1971. Photo from The Picture newspaper 11-14-71.

A FEW TRADITIONAL RAILROAD FAMILIES

McDaniel   *   Wells   *   Weatherby   *   Woodall   *   Willis *Barnes   *
McCorkle   *   Rutland   *   Kersey   *   Gurley * Reed * Cox * Cason   *
Grider   *   Wimberly   *   Beasley * Staples   *

Short   Sanders

Kelly   Austin

Pipkin   Pegram

King   Smith

Davis   Rosson

Blasingame   Kimbrough

Haynes   Dixon

(Jimmy Foster Edwards, born 9-21-42, son of Cecil & Ruby Edwards,
Cecil was a Southern Railway engineer. Photo courtesy Jimmy Edwards,
another Southern Railway engineer.)

Pittman   Davis

Wright   Huddleston
Porter * Hackworth * Edwards * Bradley * Wilson * Malone * Peters

Thompson * Crawford * Freeman * Martin *

Memories of Good Old Steam Days

What railroad man can keep their mind from going back,
When people lived along the track,
Working small fields and gardens, picking up coal in cotton sacks.
Hobos along the way, looking for a train ride, something to eat
or a place to stay.
People all seemed happy, waving at train crews.
Small children walking around in winter, barefoot, no shoes.
Steam engines seemed to fascinate them all.
The old, middle aged or even the small.
Seeing the firebox flash in middle of the night.
Reflection from the old headlight.
The old steam engine, getting slow on a hill.
Fireman shoveling coal with all his skill.
Engineer checking his train orders, also watching the rail.
He will make the schedule before him, he will do it without fail.
Running by timetable, train orders, no radio.
If you made a close run, everyone would know.
Whistle screaming, what a beautiful sound.
Drivers turning faster on every round.
Speeding through sleet, snow, sunshine or rain.
Nothing will ever replace the old steam train.
Run a water tank, trying to make up time.
Trying to out run the passenger train, closing in behind.
All these good memories, will forever be in our minds.
I wish it were possible for me to make another run with
engineer Pinkley and steam engine 6299.

This is Southern Rwy. engineer F. P. Pinkley who was promoted Dec. 12, 1937 and Maynard Kimbrough's teacher. Engine 6299 was recognized for having the most melodious sounding whistle.

Perhaps ever since the first fire was built beneath a steam locomotive boiler, the engineer has been the symbol of all railroad men. His eagle eyes pierced the storm and saw the farthest horizons. The friendly wave of the engineer and the lonesome sound of the steam whistle offered irresisrible invitations to many venturesome boys who hungered for something more interesting and challenging than a tedious life behind the plow and work on a farm.

Most railroaders exhibited a company loyalty and were careful to protect their employer's interest. At the same time, the company had an interest in their employees. A goodly part of the satisfaction arose from the belief that the job they performed was worthwhile and necessary. The steam railroaders saw some rough days in their endeavors. They were instrumental in the vast development of the area between Memphis and Chattanooga, TN. Photo in Jack Daniel Collection.

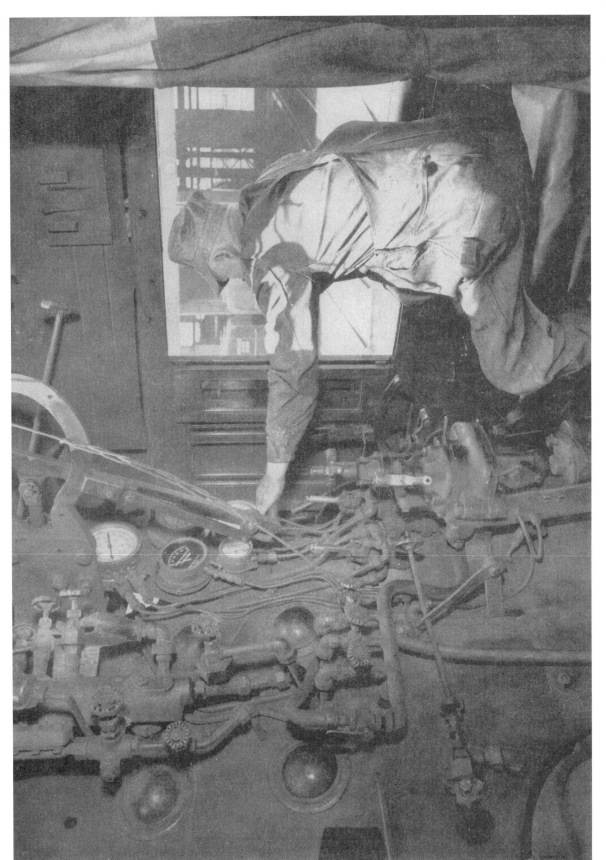

Diesels made some things automatic that were once the test of skill and understanding of the steam locomotive. Computers, electronic control systems and the nature of internal combustion have made engineers, like the one above, legendary and heroic figures of another time. This is not to say that the brothers of today will not become legendary figures in their time. Photo courtesy of The Association of American Railroads, in Jack Daniel collection.

Gone are the days of the caboose where the conductor acted as an "EOT" (end of train device). This experienced conductor used his cap to help make his signal more visable to the engineer who was probably about 40 to 50 cars away. These hands for train communication would be impossible with today's long trains. Photo by the late Horace Bristol.

Those early childhood stories about the Little Red Caboose and the Little Engine That Could could probably be credited with helping develop the railroad enthusiast. To most people, the steam locomotive and the red caboose represented the railroad. Perhaps that was because they were so visible in so many locations. Nothing else quite so effectively captivated the imagination as those two things, not even the cowboy or Washington at Valley Forge. The railroad enthusiast's love for trains would have been deepened if they had been privy to conversations and tales of railroaders like the ones in this picture were probably having. We pay tribute to those "homes-away-from-home" for the conductor and flagman of yesterday. We miss seeing you ! Photo by Richard Steinheimer. Used with permission.

Memphis Division engineer James Love Wimberly standing in front of local passenger train No. 35 with engine 1471 at Cherokee, AL around 1943. Mr. Wimberly had on the typical attire of a locomotive engineer in the days of steam. The editor borrowed a camera and captured this scene which is a treasured photo of his collection. Love was born in Stevenson, AL and attended the William & Emma Austin College at Stevenson. He was hired as a fireman on August 30, 1904, promoted to engineer on August 25, 1907. He retired November 30, 1946 and moved to Birmingham, AL where he died March 26, 1950. His forty-two year career ended in the heyday of steam and I don't believe he ever ran a diesel locomotive. He had a good record as an engineer and was noted for his ability to make up time in case his train was running behind schedule. Stevenson produced the most railroaders for Southern Railway outside the Shoals Area with the Chewalla Area running close behind. Photo by Jack Daniel.

R. K. Thorne, brakeman (8-22-43) on front of locomotive 6318 and Waldo Wright, flagman (5-4-42) standing on ground at Rossville, TN in 1948. Photo courtesy R. K. Thorne.

Left to right- R. K. Thorne, brakeman (8-22-43), James Raymond ("Goat") Russell, engineer (1-17-23) and G. S. Stanley, fireman (4-26-43) beside locomotive 6318 in 1948 at Rossville, TN. Photo courtesy of R. K. Thorne.

Left to right - G. S. Stanley, fireman (4-26-43), Waldo Wright, flagman (5-4-42) and R. K. Thorne, brakeman (8-22-43) with 6318 at trips end at Forrest Yard in Memphis, TN in 1948. The conductor for this trip was R. L. "Bob" Pittman. Photo courtesy of R. K. Thorne.

On left is conductor Joseph Edgar "Ed" Dixon with Raymond K. Thorne, flagman on train 35 between Chattanooga, TN and Sheffield, AL. Photo courtesy of R. K. Thorne.

Moving forward to 1982, this is Raymond K. Thorne, flagman on a steam excursion. R. K. retired soon after this trip. Photo courtesy of R. K. Thorne.

On left is conductor Herman P. "Big Dip" Kiser with R. K. Thorne acting as baggagemaster on this 1982 steam excursion. Photo courtesy of R. K. Thorne.

Southern Railway System

OPERATING DEPARTMENT

Sheffield, Alabama
April 25, 1947 obl/s

R. K. Thorne, Brakeman
c/o Yard Office
Sheffield, Alabama

     I am advised that you were head brakeman on No. 55, April 24, and when Fireman O. M. Rutland was injured you fired the engine to Buntyn, thereby avoiding delay to this train.

     Your service in this connection is greatly appreciated and I wish to commend you for it.

     I am placing a copy of this letter on your personal record file.

                            Superintendent

Cy - Personal Record

R. K. Thorne did not necessarily want this letter to be included in this book but the editor felt it was interesting and worthy of an explanation. Engineer John E. King (promoted 4-11-42) and fireman Oscar M. Rutland (entered service 2nd time 12-27-43) and R. K., head brakeman were on train No. 55 and at Cypress, TN, mile post 472.5, when fireman Rutland fell from the locomotive which was going about 35 miles per hour. Fortunately, there were no major injuries. The editor doesn't remember any other such incident happening on the Memphis Division. Information provided by R. K. Thorne.

Pictured here is Southern Railway locomotive 6301 getting ready for 1st No. 51 at Sheffield, AL yards in the 1940s with fireman Melvin Holland, on left, and engineer Albert Crawford, Sr., on right. The two photos on this page were made by Edith Crawford, wife of Albert, and were given to the editor. Mrs. Edith Crawford was 92 years young on October 21, 1997 and still enjoys a good memory. The editor salutes her. Photo in Jack Daniel Collection.

From another angle, this same 1st No. 51 with locomotive 6301 is getting ready for departure for Memphis, TN. Engineer Albert Harold Crawford, Sr. is on ground and Melvin Holland is on top left. The fellow in center is believed to be R. W. Laughlin, trainman. Identity of other trainman is not known. The Crawfords had a son, Albert Harold Crawford, Jr. who was an engineer and another son, Gerald Crawford, who was an operator and was stationed in Grand Junction when he died. Photo in Jack Daniel Collection.

34

Southern Railway 1st No. 51 engine 6301 has a head of steam and black smoke for engineer Albert Crawford as they climb Lily Pond Hill in Tuscumbia (Valdosta), AL. Albert Crawford lived about two miles, as the crow flies, from this location and he would blow his famous "Whippoorwill" on the whistle to let his wife know he was on his way out. This photo also shows how well the section gangs maintained the track and right-of-way. Note how the weeds have been scraped off and what a neat straight line the ballast was kept. Photo courtesy of Edith Crawford and in Jack Daniel Collection.

Col. Harland Sanders keenly remembered his days on the Southern when he lived in Tuscumbia, AL and fired on the Northern Alabama Division in the early 1900s. The Colonel got his chance to relive his experiences during a steam excursion from Sheffield to Huntsville in the 1970s. Left to right, James A. Bistline, Southern's assistant vice president, the Colonel and Fred Black , an engineer who acted as fireman. Photo in Jack Daniel Collection.

BRO. R. J. WILSON.

Caught Wild Turkey with Locomotive. Tuscumbia, AL Dec. 23, 1912. To Editor BLE Journal. Enclosed please find pcture of Bro. Robert J. Wilson, of Division 423, and clipping which tells of his catch while making fast time on his regular run. Bro. Wilson is at present our local chairman, and one of the most trusted passenger engineers on the Southern. He has been on this division since 1876, coming here from the Norfolk & Western. He entered the service as an engine wiper, then fireman, and was promoted to engineer in 1879. He has always had a clear record with no wrecks of any kind. He has two sons who are on the way and ambitious to become engineers like their father.The clipping alluded to says: "Bob Wilson, passenger engineer on the Memphis Division of Southern, who runs from Memphis to Tuscumbia, AL ran into a flock of 40 wild turkeys near Cypress, TN. Killed 3 and captured one which got caught in the pilot. Bob says the turkeys did not seem to realize their danger until the train was upon them and thinks it wonderful that not more of them were killed. Fraternally yours, S. M. Hall, Div. 423

A favorite expression of Roy E. McCorkle's is "lets talk about the old cabbage days." The cabbage days were days of Pullmans, VIP passengers and everybody in town meeting the train. "Now, all up and down the line they're tearing down the depots." He is 72 years old (1966) and more than three fourths of his life was spent in service to Southern Railway. McCorkle started working at the roundhouse in Sheffield in 1911 and on September 7, 1912 went on the road as fireman. He was promoted to engineer in 1918 and became a freight engineer on a regular basis in 1937. From 1953 to the first day of this year (1966), he was passenger engineer on two runs, Sheffield to Memphis and Sheffield to Chattanooga. "When I started, a day's work was 12 hours, with an hour off for lunch and the pay was a dollar and a dime," he said. Firing used to be one of the meanest jobs on the road, now it is the easiest." He remembers pulling a meal sack over his head when he opened the fire door which was on a chain and would stay open. That was before stokers and air-doors. It took about 23 or 24 tons of coal per trip. His wife, the former Grace Spurgeon - whose father and grandfather were railroad men - laughs about the way he used to come home with his face all black and sooty and how he always wanted his overalls starched until they could stand up on the floor. "We wound up with diesels and it's just like stepping from a wagon into an automobile." Very few accidents mar McCorkle's long record, but he did have a few and one of these was very unusual in nature. This is how he described it: "I was coming down Iuka Hill when a man drove three yoke of oxen onto the track. The wagon was loaded with sawmill logs. There was no way to prevent it. I plowed right into it, scattered logs everywhere. Killed all the steers. The man must have been pretty scared. He ran off and we never did see him. Riding a diesel is the finest thing for an old man. It's just like sitting in your own livingroom. You have fans, windshield wipers and everything." He recalls that it used to take 14 to 16 hours to get to Memphis with the old steam engines. One of the McCorkle daughters, Alice, is married to Denzil Sockwell, who is freight agent at Decatur, AL. Another daughter, Martha Sue Fleming, is manager of a Holiday Inn at Huntsville. Their son, Robert is with Young & Pittman (1966). From an interview with Lorene Frederick, staff writer, The Florence Times - Tri Cities Daily Newspaper.(* Editor's note - Robert married Marciel Miller who was a former neighbor of mine at Cherokee, Al.)

Mrs. Grace McCorkle died December 28, 1998 at the age of 100.

Pictured here are Cecil Edwards (entered service 12-14-39 and promoted to engineer 10-13-43) and his brother, Jimmy W. Edwards, Jr. (entered service 8-31-37 and promoted to engineer 10-12-42) standing by Southern 6316 near Sheffield, AL roundhouse.

Jimmy W. Edwards, Jr. in cab of Southern Railway 6316. The lettering under the cab window does not show specifications for the engine. Usually down in the right hand corner beneath the Memphis division designation would be markings like, Ms 63 24/30 85 which meant Ms for Mikado type engine, 63 for size of driving wheels, 24 over 30 for size of stroke and cylinders and the 85 for length of engine and tender. Photo provided by J. W. Edwards, Jr., retired.

These Southern Railway veterans of many years are shown here at the Muscle Shoals Railroad Museum in the former Muscle Shoals, AL depot for the 1973 Railroad Week are; left to right, Roy McCorkle, W. Dave Shrader, Percy Ricks and Bob McCord, all engineers. Photo from Colbert County Reporter, September 27, 1973.

Pictured here are other Southern Railway veterans attending Railroad Week celebration. Left to right, Jim Maples, engineer, Floyd Wilson, yard engineer, Hyman Pannel, yard switchman, Bovel Hargett, engineer, Lon Wells, engineer, C. H. Wilson, yard fireman and later ran concession stand at Muscle Shoals depot, Lance Brown and Bob McCord, engineer. Photo in Colbert County Reporter, September 27, 1973.

Captured in this 1976 photo were, left to right, S. Harry Young, Jr., Southern conductor (promoted 11-14-42), Fred Black, Southern engineer (promoted 10-4-64) and Jimmy Edwards, Jr.,Southern engineer (promoted 10-12-42). Photo courtesy of Jimmy Edwards.

Even though Southern Railway crew members received calls soon after their rest was up during World War II, Cecil Edwards, Southern engineer (promoted 10-13-43) on left and Vernon Rudder, Southern engineer (promoted 12-4-42) on right, found a little time to get some fishing in. These young railroaders, at the time, may have taken a few days off. Photo courtesy of Jimmy Edwards.

Veteran Southern Railway employees seemed to enjoy working on the steam powered excursions. Pictured here is engineer John Hubert McWilliams of Tuscumbia, AL (entered service 12-23-40, promoted 4-2-45) who engineered a May 2, 1982 trip with engine 2716. Photo by Jack Daniel

One steam powered trip had to have a diesel substitute. Pictured here is veteran engineer, Jimmy Edward (entered service 8-31-37, promoted 10-12-42) from Sheffield, AL, on right. Next to him was a railroader from the Mississippian Railroad, Jim Carlisle, from Amory, MS who came up to see steam engine number 77 which had been purchased from his road by the Muscle Shoals Railroad Club. He joined engineer Edwards along with fireman B. W. Wells(not pictured here) for a portion of the round trip from Sheffield, AL to Corinth, MS and return. Photo by Jack Daniel.

40

L to R - Bernard Couch, engineer (12-22-40), Walter W. Thompson, brakeman (8-27-43) and R. K. Thorne, flagman (8-22-43) on the EMCO turn. The EMCO run is from Sheffield, AL Yard to several industrial plants in the Shoals Area, then returned to yard. Photo courtesy R. K. Thorne.

The old and the new meet at Corinth, MS in the 1980's. Two things in the background are long gone; the motor car to the right of the diesel and a red and white GM&O diesel back behind the Southern diesel. Photo by Jack Daniel, editor.

A painting of Albert H. Crawford, Sr. and Melvin Holland on first No. 51 at Sheffield Yard in the 1940s. The artist was a McWilliams and the work looks very much like the two. Photo of painting courtesy of Blaine W. Wells, a retired Southern Railway engineer.

Sheffield, AL yard crews getting ready for work in the late 1940s. L to R; J. C. Reed, (switchman entered service 6-14-43) - Vester L. Everett, (entered service 2-24-46) - Hugh L. Robinson (switchman, entered service 9-14-41) - W. C. Huddleston (clerk 8-18-42) - Blaine W. Wells (fireman 9-29-49) - Eric N. Gibson (switchman 12-14-45) - Ray R. Kennedy (switchman 11-14-40) - back of Tom Morris (engineer 12-23-15) - Paul Rice (switchman 10-5-42) - J. Harold Stansell (switchman 10-16-41) - J. E. "Fisty" Westbrook (fireman 1-3-45) - Photo courtesy of Blaine Wells, retired engineer.

An Engineers Warning

As we run a locomotive, we see many things along the way.
We see the sad and lonely, the happy and carefree.
We see the school bus, as it carries children to school.
The farmer with the tractor or maybe plowing the mule.
We observe the road before us, watch motorist along the way.
They are the ones that chill us and sometimes we often pray,
That they will be more cautious and realize how helpless we are.
As you approach the railroad crossing, you seem to think we can
stop like a car.
Yes, we see you come up the highway, you seem to observe
highway warnings well.
Then you will cross our railroad crossings, you seem to ignore
our warnings, the lights, whistle and bell.
We have the crossing warning, stop signs and light.
You seem not to heed them, nor have any fear nor fright.
Let me say to you motorists, whether old or young.
We make the same attempt to save you, as if it were our wife
daughter or son.
If you could once ride beside us and realize the weight that is behind.
That shoves this big locomotive, you would know that stopping takes time.
We think you would tell others, how helpless we engineers are.
That would make them more careful, before they enter our crossing
with their car.
If you would only wait a matter of minutes, we the crossing to you will give.
Instead of being killed, hurt or mangled, many of you would live.
So all you motorists take my warning, use common sense and fear.
I know these things are a reality, for I have seen many of them,
you see I am an engineer.

Maynard Kimbrough

Written in 1968
Maynard Kimbrough
Retired Southern Railway Engineer

Flood water covers Southern Railroad at Pocahontas, TN on February 14, 1948. Photo by John Dunbar in Jack Daniel Collection.

Back in the five-man crew days, standing beside Southern Railway locomotive 6312 at Sheffield, AL are and were some of the Memphis Division's finest railroaders. Left to right are; O. O. Osborn, trainman who entered service 8-31-42 and promoted to conductor 10-21-66 - Marvin Kimbrough, fireman who entered service 5-2-42 and promoted to engineer 3-11-62 - William Scott Jones, conductor who entered service 6-25-17 and promoted to conductor 3-2-26 - Fred Paul Pinkley, engineer who entered service 12-6-18 as fireman and promoted to engineer 12-12-37 - Herman P. Kiser, trainman who entered service 5-14-41 and promoted to conductor 12-18-48. Photo courtesy of Marvin Kimbrough who is retired and produces a fine garden each year.

Southern Railway's Sheffield, Alabama shops employed many people during the 1920s, 30s, 40s and 50s. Crafts such as : blacksmiths, boilermakers, electricians, painters, car repairers, shop laborers, welders and machinists. A few that could be identified here were: Jim DuBois, Dave Staples, Floyd McCorkle, E. H. Inman, Arthur Dillahunty, Henry Hanlin, Julius Fischer and Ernest Nelson. Photo courtesy of Mrs. Jimmy Edwards, daughter of E. H. Inman.

HERBERT R. MEADOWS

Many Southern Railway and Norfolk Southern railroaders remember Herbert Meadows as a Southern Railway conductor. Herb entered service on June 9, 1944 as a brakeman, promoted to conductor on October 29, 1966 and retired in 1985. Retired from the railroad that is. Herb is now 80 years young and is pictured here with his wife, Arliss, in their East Pasadena Avenue yard in Muscle Shoals, AL. Herb and Arliss were awarded the Beautification Award for the summer season by the Muscle Shoals Beautification Committee for their beautiful yard, which also contains an American flag on a pole.

Herb and his friend Maynard Kimbrough, a retired Southern Railway engineer, get together for coffee most every day, except when they might be making a trip to see their kids in Texas or Georgia. Not thinking, one of herb's daughters asked him one time what he and Maynard talked about at coffee breaks. This question astounded Herb. "Why dear, we run trains, lots of them and we come back home with no cinders down our shirt collar either." Herb has a very distinctive voice, one that can't be forgotten and one that belongs to him alone. We hope those voices can be heard for many more pleasurable years.

It is not unusual for a railroader to come from a lineage of railroaders with many members of the family working for the railroad. This is true in Herb's case as his grandfather, John Daniel "Bud" Meadows, was a conductor on the Memphis & Charleston Railroad back when the road only ran east from Memphis to Burns (Burnsville), MS. That was because bridges had not been built over Yellow Creek and Bear Creek. There was a turntable at Burns so the trains could be turned and return to Memphis.When the bridges were completed, Mr. Meadows moved from Burnsville to Tuscumbia. At the time John Daniel Meadows was working, there was a very prominent M&C conductor by the name of Harry Ryan who was a Captain in the Confederate Army during the Civil War. Captain Ryan was the Military Aide in charge of day to day operations of the M&C during the war. Captain Ryan also introduced the train order system for the M&C. After the war, he returned to the road as a conductor as he wanted to be out there with his old friends, which no doubt included John Daniel Meadows.

John Daniel Meadows named a son Harry Ryan Meadows. Harry Ryan Meadows was Herb Meadow's father. Thereby we had a grandfather-grandson railroad family. Herb's dad ran a grocery store in Tuscumbia, AL and in the latter years of his life he sold seed and bought cotton in Tuscumbia.

The editor wishes to pay tribute to Herb's grandfather and to Herb and Maynard Kimbrough for not retiring from life but continuing to be active. However, the editor tends to believe that Arliss might be the one with the green thumb and responsible for the beautiful flowers.Herb say's no. Photo in Jack Daniel Collection.

Maynard Kimbrough and wife Dorothy. Maynard and Herb Meadows have coffee together practically every day where much of their conversation got around to railroading. The poems that appear later in the book were written by Maynard. I have tried many many times to get an old retired "hoghead" to write down some of his experiences and stories about his career. After nagging Maynard several times, he finally jotted down some information. I have always found that the old steam railroaders can remember engine numbers and the crews that they were with pretty well. That is a mark of a dedicated railroad man. Jack Daniel, editor.

Maynard Kimbrough

I hired out as a fireman for the Southern Railway on December 16, 1939 which was just prior to World War II. The steam locomotives were hand-fired in those days. It required shovelling from twenty-four to thirty-one tons of coal per trip from Sheffield to Chattanooga or Memphis. I must point out that you called your shovel a scoop on the railroad. There were coal chutes located at Sheffield, Paint Rock and deButts yard at Chattanooga and on west-end at Corinth and Forrest yard in Memphis. The fireman could clean his fire at Decatur, Huntsville and Stevenson on east-end and Corinth and Grand Junction on the west-end. There were water tanks at Sheffield, Wheeler, Decatur, Huntsville, Larkinsville, and one at Shellmound on the NC&StL (This track is no longer there as it was rerouted because of the backwater on Nickajack Dam.) On the west-end, there were water tanks at Margerum, Corinth, Cypress, Grand Junction and Forrest yard.

As a cub or student fireman, you had to watch such things as a water glass and steam gauge, keeping a level fire and be particular about corners and side sheets and not to "short fire" and don't throw in large chunks of coal and things such as that. I made my first cub trip as fireman with engineer Lon Wells, who had been promoted November 1, 1937, and fireman C. L. Smith, who had hired out October 27, 1925, and we had steam locomotive No 4514. These fellows were nice to me and took time to show me the art of firing and the rules of railroading and safety. One had to get approval of six engineers before the cub could then be on his own and make the extra board.

After I had finished my cubbing, I made my first pay trip with engineer Joe Hackworth, who had been promoted to engineer May 27, 1913, and we had engine 6312 on December 16, 1939. Mr. Joe was also good to me and we made a good trip and made a Stevenson turnout of Chattanooga on this trip. I was nervous on my first trip as fireman as I wasn't sure that I could keep the engine hot. After that first trip as fireman, my nerves seemed to settle down and I could relax a little more. We soon learned which engines were poor steamers or good steamers. All engines steamed a little different and you had to fire them differently. In the early forties, the engines began to have stokers installed in them at the Knoxville shops. This meant that the coal was fed into the boiler by mechanical means and eliminated the back-breaking hand firing.

I didn't work the extra board very long before I got a regular job firing for F. P. Pinkley, who had been promoted to engineer December 12, 1937, whom I considered one of the best engineers on the Memphis Division. This man was patient with me and treated me like a son. He taught me everything he knew about a steam locomotive and all the extra things about becoming a reliable engineer. He would let me get first hand experience by letting me run the engine on my own while he observed me and pointed out things a good engineer should know. I shall always remember this great railroader for extending his knowledge to me.

I was promoted to engineer on July 1, 1944 and made my first trip on engine 6305 with George Dillon, who entered service on June 15, 1944, as my fireman and J. Felix Castleberry, who had entered service on July 10, 1918, as my conductor. We were on train No. 52, a fast freight. I was not nervous on this trip because I had gained confidence through the great people who had taught me about steam locomotives.

My first assigned job as engineer was on the Stevenson Pusher with Marcus Everett Crabtree, who had entered service on September 9, 1942, as fireman and Walter Talley Cox, who had entered service on July 30, 1918, as conductor. We were stationed at Stevenson for six weeks and were on call by the Sheffield dispatcher. I remember the trains that we assisted over "Big Coon" mountain were longer than I was used to running. There was an all-night cafe at Stevenson that sure did come in handy for coffee and food. I looked on this job as a valuable experience.

The first diesels on the Memphis Division were used on The Tennessean. In the beginning, the fireman on this job often had to run through both ends of the division because there were not enough trained men on the diesel. These passenger trains would reach speeds of 90 miles per hour where stretches of track permitted. I think back to the time when 25 and 26 pulled passenger trains with a running time of three hours thirty-five minutes with four regular stops and one flag stop. Freight train 52 had a hot freight running time from Buntyn to Sheffield of four hours fifty minutes. We have left Buntyn thirty or forty minutes ahead of No. 26 and we knew that a delay to 26 was a no no but we never left a stop or approach board for it. Almost all engine crews longed for the day they had whiskers enough (seniority) to bid-in and get the job on the Memphis Special, later named The Tennessean.

I think one of the most pleasant memories of the steam locomotive was the whistle blowing and at night, when the firedoor was opened, the ray of light flashing into the sky. We all thought that engine 6299 had the most beautiful whistle. I have been on it going down through Chewalla and Pocahontas with the whistle blowing and watch the colored section gangs take off their cap and reach down as if they were dusting the rails ahead of us. Those section boys just couldn't control their actions as the whistle did something deep down in their souls. To tell you the truth, it sent chills down my spine also.

My final run as engineer was May 8, 1982 on steam locomotive 2716 that Southern Railway had leased from the Kentucky Railroad Museum to use to power the steam passenger excursions. This was the largest engine that I ever operated. We had 19 cars and ran from Huntsville to Chattanooga and then back to Sheffield. Besides my family being on board, the National Geographic camera crews were on board filming for their organization. I am thankful that I was able to retire on the same kind of power that I began. I was also able to go off duty at the same place I began 43 years earlier, at the Sheffield yard office. I remember the old Sheffield yard office telephone number was 405.

So many of my friends have departed this life. I want to express appreciation to the former Southern Railway and now the Norfolk Southern for employing me those many hard but pleasurable years riding the rails. My son, Don, became a railroader too. His picture appears on the next page as well as pictures of two engineers who helped me along the way,

Don Kimbrough, son of Maynard and Dorothy Kimbrough. Don worked for Southern and Norfolk Southern as track supervisor, assistant trainmaster, superintendent of terminals and for four years as superintendent of the Pocahontas division, where they won three consecutive system-wide safety awards, before being named recently as general manager of the Eastern Region in Atlanta.

Two Southern Railway engineers that Maynard Kimbrough remembers helping him in his career. On left is Fred Paul Pinkley and on right is Joseph Randolph Hackworth, both locomotive engineers.

Final Run

It was May 8, 1982
I made my final run and I realized I was through.
This day brought back many memories of engineers who helped me.
One in particular, Pinkley, whose initials were F. P.
He took time with me as if I were his son,
Taught me the way to really make those steam engines run.
I used it all through the years we had our steam.
Really made me feel good, seemed like a dream.
Having all our family to ride with me on this final run,
As we left Huntsville, thrills and memories begun.
I also knew that I must do the best I could,
As I prayed many times I would.
Don & Dan with camera, video along highway with me.
We are looking forward, all this to hear and see.
Thinking of the hundreds of passengers whose lives were in my hands.
Many from all parts of our land.
All my family was looking to me to do well with this train.
I had done this many times, I knew I could again.
Marvin was my fireman, he knew how to feed the coal,
That made plenty steam to make this big engine roll.
When I reached Chattanooga on this run,
Was greeted by my entire family, granddaughter and grandsons.
We made it to Chattanooga about on time.
I had 170 miles left, retirement would be mine.
My wife was riding the train, my helper good and true.
She is responsible for my success, years over forty-two.
We left Chattanooga to make Sheffield we must do.
To make this long trip was in doubt by my own crew.
I knew I could make it if all my signals were green.
To see them this color was a pretty scene.
We made it to Huntsville, eight-thirty to be exact.
The officials mounted the engine and presented me with a plaque.
My children rode the engine, they knew this was the last.
I wanted them to see, I was still the engineer I had been in the past.
Donna rode in the seat behind me.
We made it to the terminal, the thrill was all mine.
To go off duty at the same place I started in '39.
One passenger was absent, I wish he could have ridden with me.
That's my teacher Pinkley whose initials were F. P.
Yes, my teacher was absent who treated me as a son,
But you would have been proud of your student, on this final run.

Maynard Kimbrough - Retired Southern Railway Engineer - Written in 1982.

Some Bygone Memories

Returning from Knoxville, we stopped by the Chattanooga Choo-Choo.
It made me kinda blue.
Seeing the changes that have been made in the last twenty years.
At times could hardly hold back tears.
The tracks we used to back in and pull out on passenger trains.
If we could only see those days again.
The station where passengers and less fortunate came off street to stay,
Is now made into a cafe.
Some of the tracks we used at all hours,
Are removed and now growing beautiful flowers.
Some of the Pullmans that were ridden in depression, wartime and boom,
Are now rented as hotel rooms.
The Ellis Restaurant, that used to be one of the best,
Is now closed like all the rest.
The St. George and Hotel Grand,
Closed silent, vacant, still stand.
The streets we used to walk at anytime,
Is almost untravelled by foot, because of crime.
The station master room, where we received orders, consist of cars,
Is now open as a bar.
The room where we stayed on short stops,
Is now opened as a novelty shop.
Though the old benches, where we used to sit and rest,
Are still intact, like all the rest.
Inside that used to be main lobby, is now a dining area.
Places to eat most everywhere.
I'm thankful they let this passenger station stand.
It has accomodated people from all over our land.
Passenger trains will never come into this station again.
I can still remember the good days when,
As a fireman or engineer, I saw people greeting or saying goodbye.
In those days on passenger trains you could rely.
These times have passed us by, things are different and new.
Still lots of mixed emotions comes from visiting the "Choo-Choo."

by Maynard Kimbrough - written in 1986

Clyde Berry - Dispatcher (1986)

I graduated high school at Colbert County High in Leighton, AL in 1946 and immediately entered the Navy. I served my country for two years and became a civilian again in 1948. I planned to enter Florence State Teachers College (now University of North Alabama) to take up studies for a career. Before the term started, my cousin, Aubrey Smith, approached me one day and asked me if I would be interested in telegraphy and learning the Morse Code. At the time, I wasn't particularly interested. I was becoming bored with nothing to do. I agreed to accept the practice telegraph set and Aubrey wrote down the Morse Code for me. I accompanied Aubrey to his work a few times at Decatur, AL and Iuka, MS just to have something to do. At that time, I had no thoughts about railroad service.

About two months later, Aubrey called me and said that A. H. "Buddy" Thompson, chief dispatcher for Southern Railway at Sheffield, AL wanted to know if I would fill-in one day for Mr. Formby, the agent-operator at Gurley, who needed to be off. I told him I didn't know "didely squat" about being an agent-operator. He assured me that he would take care of me and cover for me. He would see to it that no train orders would be issued at Gurley that day. Aubrey and Mr. Thompson made it sound so easy and simple that I thought "what-the-heck" and accepted their offer.

I went to Gurley, opened the doors and became an agent-operator. I fumbled around and occupied my time pretty well as time slipped by slowly. All of a sudden, a big guy comes in the office and told me he had loaded three cars of logs and he wanted them on the next local. I swallowed a couple of times and told him they would be on the next local. After he left, I thought to myself that these cars would probably need some kind of papers (waybills) before the local could include the cars in it's consist. I had never seen a waybill much less know how to fill one out. I fumbled enough that the local came and went, needless to say, without the three cars. To my surprise, the shipper showed up again and wanted to know why the local didn't pick up his logs. I let him know that I had told the local crew the cars were not ready because this was my first day at railroading and I didn't know what to do. He was sympathetic and understood. That was August or September of 1948 and my first taste of railroading.

When I returned to Sheffield, I was greeted with a message that Mr. Thompson wanted me to sub for the agent at Paint Rock for one week on the 11 p.m. to 7 a.m. shift. Realizing that I had survived the first day, I accepted the offer. No sooner than I had returned home this time, Mr. Thompson suggested that I needed to learn about selling tickets at the old Sheffield Depot. Mr. S. G. House was having health problems and needed to be on sick leave. I would work with Lawrence Crowson. I cubbed on this job 2 weeks and later in 1948 and the spring of 1949, I worked in place of Mr. House.

After cubbing all this time, I was placed on the extra board as an operator-ticket clerk. My first regular job was 2 shifts at Sheffield yard, 2 shifts at Sheffield ticket office and 1 shift at Decatur block office. I had jobs at Iuka, MS and Margerum, AL and a few other places but never west of Iuka nor east of Paint Rock. I spent a good bit of time with dispatchers "Cap" Ennis and Glen Bryan. They encouraged me to sit in and cub with them, which I did. In 1960 I was placed on the seniority list of telegraphers and dispatchers. I was the first dispatcher hired after World War II. They had layed off several dispatchers just after the war was over. In August, 1964, Southern Railway closed the Sheffield dispatchers office and consolidated it with Knoxville, TN. Only H. A. Carlin and myself accepted jobs in the Knoxville dispatchers office. So I became a dispatcher in Knoxville from 1964 and remained until I retired in 1990.

I worked with many Southern Railway superintendents who went on to become general managers and presidents of Southern Railway. I stayed on during Norfolk Southern days and went from issuing train orders to issuing track warrants. Train dispatching is an exacting job and requires your undivided attention. When you have trains coming from the east and west using the same main track, the best possible meeting place must be determined. In my day, I had to know something about steam locomotives and locomotive engineers. Some could make up lost time better than others. Passenger trains should not be delayed. Trains used to have designated timetable numbers and often times would be run in sections of the same number. Yes, it was interesting work and kept one on his toes.

I tried to always treat all employees with respect and in the same manner I would like to be treated. I made many enduring friendships during my career. I had many friends who worked for Southern that, when they were off duty, would go out and do favors for me in order to keep trains running. This was before radios for communication. I really appreciated the help they gave me down through the years. Railroading got in my blood, perhaps slowly in the beginning, but I soon developed into a dedicated railroad man. As they would say today, I became a seasoned and veteran railroader and I don't regret any moment of it. A great majority of my memories are pleasant ones. With the help of my wife Betty, my life, though retired, is still holding the main line and hasn't taken siding yet. We can rest assured that on "life's railway to Heaven" someone else will be doing the dispatching; Signed CWB.

A. H. "Buddy" Thompson, Chief Dispatcher
Southern Railway - Sheffield, AL

"Cap" Lawrence Ennis - Dispatcher - Southern Rwy
Sheffield, , Alabama

Retired Southern Railway employees (L to R); Aubrey Smith, agent-operator, Blaine Wells, road engineer, Maynard Kimbrough, road engineer, Clyde Berry, dispatcher and Denzil Sockwell, agent-operator. Aubrey Smith and Clyde Berry are cousins. Photo courtesy Aubrey Smith.

Aubrey Smith, freight agent at Florence, AL in 1968. Old Southern Depot now used as warehouse. Photo courtesy of Aubrey Smith.

Alice L. (Tommy) Middleton who was an agent-operator for Southern in the 1940s - 1960s. Photo courtesy of Aubrey Smith.

Pictured here is Southern Railway president, W. Graham Claytor, who was president from 1967 to 1976. Mr. Clayton was instrumental in inaugurating the steam powered specials. He also would pack a grip and take off on weekends for some division of Southern and ride the diesels to get to know the men and the territory. Photo by Jack Daniel, editor.

I don't know whether the railroads ever considered it a compliment that so many rail enthusiastic people would love trains. Some of them would lay off from work in order to get to see and photograph trains in action. Pictured here are two among thousands who were great rail potographers. On left is the late John Rea from Memphis. John had worked on a manuscript about the Memphis Street Railway. On right is John Schafer who at that time was from Memphis and worked for DuPont and now lives in Ohio. On May 3, 1983, the editor had joined the two to photograph the steam locomotive 750 which came to Memphis. Photo by Jack Daniel, editor.

Members of the Memphis Chapter of the National Railway Historical Society were dedicated to helping people enjoy a trip behind a steam powered excursion. Pictured here, left to right, is Dr. Raymond Mayer, the National Director of the Memphis Chapter and a retired physician now living in Arkansas. In the middle is D. E. Gribble who worked for the City of Memphis. To his right is his son. The editor had the pleasure to serve as President of the Memphis Chapter when Dr. Mayer was National Director. We enjoyed many train trips together. Dr. Mayer had a brother that was a conductor for Southern Railway on another division. Photo by Jack Daniel.

Other Memphians who were members of the Memphis Chapter of the National Railway Historical Society are pictured here. From left, Chester Shields, who was in his late eighties in this picture, and Bill Rudd, far right, assisted Southern Railway trainman, James Barnes, in getting passengers on and off the train. Photo by Jack Daniel.

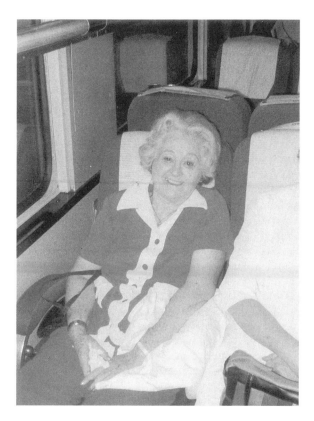

Miss Sarah Counts was a clerk for Southern. After retirement, she was confined to a wheelchair. The Muscle Shoals Railroad Club did not let that stop her from riding a steam powered excursion. Special arrangements were made and she brought along her special nurse. The smile on her face was worth all the efforts. Photo by Jack Daniel, editor.

On left is Carl F. Young, Sr., a member of the Muscle Shoals Railroad Club. On right is Grady Nixon, a Southern carryall driver in Sheffield, AL. Grady worked as a porter on this excursion train and Carl worked in the concession car. Carl, Jr. is an engineer on the Norfolk Southern. photo by Jack Daniel, editor.

Dr. John Chandler & Family

The editor wishes to pay tribute to a friend and his family, Dr. John Chandler, an orthopaedic surgeon in Memphis back in the 70's but now practices in Bristol, TN. He still remains a member of the Memphis Chapter of the National Railway Historical Society. John and I made several trips on steam excursions together. He is a railroad enthusiast and has a train layout in his basement. He probably got his interest from his grandfather who was a steam locomotive engineer for the Southern Railway on another division in one of the Carolinas. Pictured here with John, left to right, is wife Susi, sons Chris and Jeremy. Susi works part-time, paying bills for the orthopaedic practice, which now has 8 surgeons to share call with and give John a little more time with the family. Jeremy and Chris are active in scouting, cross country running, track, karate, camping and rock climbing. During the summer of 1996, the boys along with dad, participated in archery contests, bringing home several awards, while putting in many hours of practice in the back yard (on a fake deer). I am very happy to pay tribute to such an all around American family and wish for them the best. Photo in Jack Daniel collection.

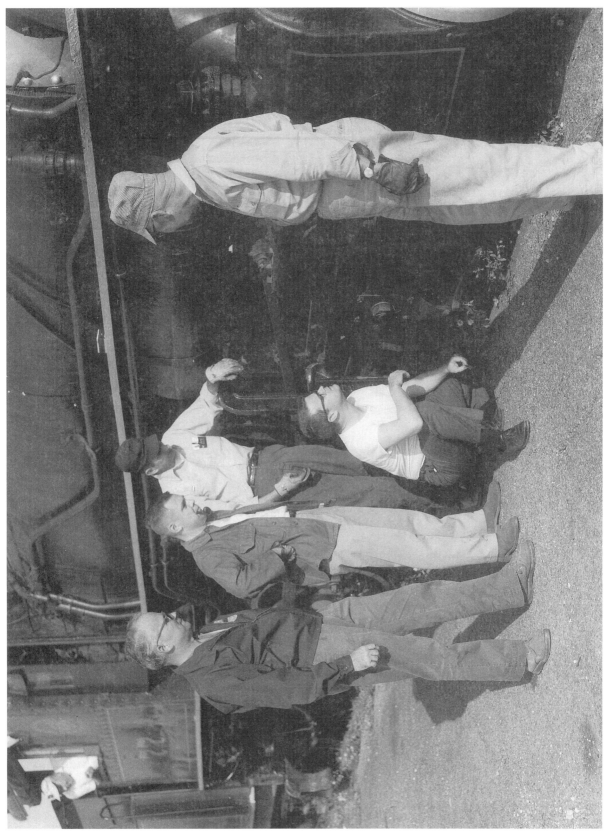

The Muscle Shoals Railroad Club owned steam locomotive # 77 and many hours of hard but enjoyable work was done on the engine to get in running condition. Pictured here in the cab is F. J. Moss, a club member and a Sheffield City policeman. He lived near where the engine was stored and he kept a watchful eye out for it. On the ground, left to right, is Hugh Dudley, a faithful member who lives in Huntsville and became president of the North Alabama Railroad Museum. Next to Hugh is member John Mabry. Next to John is Jack Daniel, the editor and who was then president of the club. Squatting down is member Jim Sims who is currently the president of the museum. Finally, the late Charlie Smith, a devoted club member. Charlie was a retired road foreman of engines for Southern Railway. Photo in Jack Daniel Collection.

Many people have heard the song "Wreck of Old 97" about the wreck that happened at Stillhouse Trestle north of Danville, VA on September 27, 1903. Many may not have seen a photo of it. Curious onlookers were on hand. It is hard to believe that locomotive # 1102 eventually was repaired and placed back in service. Photo in Jack Daniel Collection.

This three-railroad crossing is near Main Street Station in Richmond, VA and this photo was made in 1936. On the top is C&O # 433, in the middle is Seaboard Airline # 267 and on the bottom is Southern Railway # 1204. Photo in Jack Daniel Collection.

GM&O engine 458 was run on trains 57 & 58 between Corinth, MS and Memphis, TN. The trains were manned by Southern crews. Photo in Jack Daniel Collection.

This photo made in Birmingham, AL. Birmingham, like many other cities, did not preserve the station as the wrecker's ball got it down. Though the 4501 still exists, we no longer see it on mainline excursions. Gone also are two friends of the editor. On the left is Edgar Goins who worked for the Tennessee Valley Authority. In the middle, sitting on the 4501, is Herbert Sims who owned a machine shop in Florence, AL. Herbert was a member of the Muscle Shoals Railroad Club and was the father of Jim Sims, another valuable member. Mr. Sims was an excellent machinist and rebuilt parts for locomotive # 77. He donated many free hours of service to the club. Standing on the right is Jack Daniel, the editor of this book and at the time was president of the club. Photo in Jack Daniel Collection.

Memphis Union Station was a beautiful building. Memphis was not as fortunate as Nashville and Chattanooga in saving the station from the wrecker's ball. What the citizens of Memphis have in its place is the Main Postoffice Building. This station opened in 1912 and was owned by the five railroads that used it; Missouri Pacific, L&N, Cotton Belt, Southern and NC&StL Photo in University of Memphis Special Collections Library and is courtesy of Larry Thomas, editor of Terminal Railroad Association of St. Louis Historical & Technical Society. Photo in Jack Daniel Collection.

In many American towns, the depot was the most important building. The depot touched the lives of people in the community. Time ran out for most of the depots between Memphis and Chattanooga, TN. From depot to depot, America spread and developed by the rails. Pictured here is the Cherokee, AL depot built in 1857 and torn down in 1973. Photo in Jack Daniel Collection.

Tractive effort, boiler dimensions and pressure, size of drivers - these statistics enable one to judge just what a steam locomotive could do...at least on paper. Most engine-watchers had a favorite wheel arrangement based not only on performance statistics but two other factors? How does she look? How does she sound? For me, I enjoyed the melodious whistle sound of engine 6299 and thought the 1400 series of passenger engines the most beautiful and balanced looking. Southern Memphis Division 6312 was a mikado type built by Richmond in 1922, pictured here at Forrest Yard in Memphis in September, 1948. Photo in Harold Volrath collection.

Southern Railway # 6318, a Ms-1 type Mikado locomotive built by Richmond in 1922. Pictured here in Chattanooga, TN in August, 1948. This was another good steaming locomotive that was in service on the Memphis Division. Photo in Harold K. Vollrath Collection.

Southern Railway # 6301, a 2-8-2 Mikado type built by Richmond in 1922. This was a Memphis Division locomotive most of its 30 years of working life. Pictured here in Spartanburg, S. C. in August of 1950. Photo in Harold K. Vollrath Collection.

Southern Railway # 4518, a 2-8-2 Mikado type locomotive, built by Baldwin in 1911. Pictured here in Forrest Yard in September, 1948. This locomotive worked on the Memphis Division also. These type engines served for about 40 years before retirement. Photo in Harold K. Vollrath Collection.

Southern Railway # 4551, a 2-8-2 Mikado type locomotive, built by Baldwin in 1911. Pictured here in Birmingham, AL in June, 1940. This locomotive worked on the Memphis Division also. These type engines served for about 40 years before retirement. Photo in Harold K. Vollrath Collection.

Southern Railway # 1465, a Ts type Mountain locomotive built by Baldwin in 1917. Pictured here in Knoxville, TN in May, 1948. This was another beautiful green and gold locomotive that was in service on the Memphis Division. Photo in Harold K. Vollrath Collection.

Southern Railway # 1471, a Ts Mountain type built by Baldwin in 1917. Pictured here in Knoxville, TN in September, 1949. This engine often headed up trains 35 and 36 on the Memphis Division in the 1940s. These were the newest passenger locomotives Southern owned. In the latter days of steam, these beautiful green and gold engines could be seen heading up freights or in yard service. They all had deep-toned whistles and one could not identify the engine number by the sound of the whistle. Elsewhere in this book is a photo of engineer Love Wimberly standing in front of 1471 at Cherokee, AL. Photo in Harold K. Vollrath Collection.

74

Southern Railway # 1465, a 4-8-2 Ts Mountain type locomotive, built by Baldwin in 1917. Pictured here in Knoxville, TN in January, 1950. Knoxville's Ts pool also handled Memphis Division trains. These light Mountains were used between Chattanooga and Sheffield on trains 7 and 8 (the old Joe Wheeler) and trains 35 and 36 between Chattanooga and Memphis. Southern's Coster Shops in Knoxville were responsible for maintaining the Memphis Division power pool. This type locomotive served for about 35 years before retirement. Photo in Harold K. Vollrath Collection.

Southern Railway # 1319, a 4-6-2 Ps-2 Pacific type locomotive built by Baldwin in 1910. Pictured here in Memphis, TN in December, 1937. These passenger engines had deep-doned whistles. Photo in Harold K. Vollrath Collection.

Southern Railway # 1221, a 4-6-2 Ps Pacific type locomotive built by Baldwin in 1904. Pictured here in Memphis, TN in May, 1935. Photo in Harold K. Vollrath Collection.

Southern Railway # 1320, a 4-6-2 Ps-2 Pacific type locomotive built by Baldwin in 1910. Pictured here in Memphis Union Station in June, 1940. Photo in Harold K. Vollrath Collection.

Southern Railway # 1204, a 4-6-2 Ps-2 Pacific type locomotive built by Baldwin in 1903. Pictured here in Forrest Yard in May, 1935. Photo in Harold K. Vollrath Collection.

Southern Railway # 1307, a 4-6-2 Ps-2 Pacific type locomotive built by Baldwin in 1910. Pictured here in Memphis, TN in April of 1940. The identity of the fireman pictured in the cab is not known. Photo in Harold K. Vollrath Collection.

79

Southern Railway # 1212, a 4-6-2 Ps Pacific type locomotive built by Baldwin in 1904. This was a passenger locomotive but often was seen in freight service doubleheading with a sister engine # 1346 during World War II. They were nicknamed "The Gold Dust Twins." The front steps and handrail were missing when this photo was made in Birmingham, AL in June of 1948. Photo in Harold K. Vollrath Collection.

Southern Railway # 1746, an 0-8-0 switcher was an A-7 type built by Lima Locomotive Works in 1914. Pictured here in Forrest Yard in Memphis, TN in September, 1948. Anybody recognize the engineer? Photo in Harold K. Vollrath Collection.

Supplemental Section

This is a picture album, perhaps a welcome sight and worthy of our attention. These are vestiges of an era with faces and things familiar to some and unfamiliar to others.

Railroading is a grand, noisy spectacle, and we tend to emphasize action, inevitably overlooking some gentler traditions. Here we try to be unconventional and use people as subjects. It could be the engineer or fireman in the cab or just a guy working around the engine. It could be just a simple reminder of some other phase of railroading or hopefully just some scene that appeals to you.

Photo by Richard Berg

Photo Bland Osborn

The motorcar was used to transport telephone & signal maintainers and section crews.

Photo Ties Magazine

Ease her back that far so we can see the problem.

Photo Ties Magazine

Memphis Division conductor Herman Kiser shares something with Bill Purdie during an excursion.

Welders were certainly needed for repair jobs on the railroad.

These are Southern Railway Spencer Shop men who were proud of their work even though it was dirty & greasey. Photo David Driscoll/SRHA collection.

86

Photo Steve Patterson

Southern Railway's Memphis Division was a single-track mainline and required westbound trains to go "in the hole" for eastbound trains

87

Photo Fred Matthews

Steam locomotives required lots of water and coal to produuce the steam and firemen had to give the old girls a drink every so often.

88

Photo Jim Shaughnessy

This brakeman is taking advantage of a wait on a meet probably wishing the meet would hurry and come along so his train could get underway again.

89

LOOK AHEAD·LOOK SOUTH

Photo David Plowden

Southern Railway Memphis Division firemen got to view the countryside from the cab. There was plenty of kudzu along the Mississippi & Tennessee rights-of-way.

Photo Don Spiro

Early morning shot of Southern 4501 ready for an excursion.

The tools of the small-town operator's trade are evident here. The telegraph sounder, telescoping phone, the hooded lamp over the desk - all the trappings are here.

Anson Cooper

"Coop" was a veteran of World War II and was very patriotic and a Christian. When the Muscle Shoals Railroad Club ran its first excursion behind #77, Anson furnished American flags to be displayed on the locomotive. He never did railroad but was a dedicated supporter of the club and the railroads. He worked for the Tennessee Valley Authority and lived in Florence, AL where he died about two years ago. Photo in Jack Daniel collection.

Russell Carpenter

Pictured here is Russell Carpenter and wife Ruth on Sept. 9, 1998. Russell entered service of the Southern Railway some fifty-five years earlier on Sept. 6, 1943 as a clerk at Sheffield, AL. He went on to hold several management jobs including Road Foreman of Engines at Birmingham, AL. Photo by Jack Daniel.

Chapter Three

Yesterday's Railroad Forms

94

MEMO:

Southern Railway System

FAREWELL TO ENGINE 610

Texas & Pacific engine 610, which has been leased by Southern Railroad for the past 3 years, has made her last run and now next Saturday morning , January 24, 1981,will start her trip back to the 610 Foundation in Fort Worth, Texas. The Heart of Dixie Railroad Club is sponsoring a one way ferry trip as far as Memphis, TN and will be passing through your town sometime Saturday, or Sunday if you live beyond Sheffield, AL. See schedule below for time. We want you to have an opportunity to ride behind this grand old lady one more time. Remember this is a one-way ferry trip and you will be responsible for your transportation back. You can board or get off at any of the following stops. On Saturday the train will go through Cordova, Parrish, Jasper, Halleyville, Russellville and arriving in Sheffield around 3:00 p.m. The train will be there overnight and will leave for Memphis on Sunday morning at 10:30 a.m. stopping in Iuka, Corinth, Grand Junction, Collierville and arriving in Memphis around 4:00 p.m. For prices of fare see the station master at the Southern Railway depots in your town.

We hope you will take advantage of this rare opportunity to ride behind this grand old steam engine for it could very well be the very last time a steam engine will ever go that way again. Certainly not this giant. For those who may want to ride the train all the way to Memphis, the train will stay in Sheffield overnight and leave on Sunday morning at 10:30 a.m. and will arrive in Memphis around 4:00 p.m.

SCHEDULE FOR SATURDAY JANUARY 24, 1981:

Lv. Birmingham, AL	9:30 a.m.
Lv. Cordova, AL	10:45
Lv. Parrish, AL	11:15
Lv. Haleyville, AL	1:15 p.m.
Lv. Russellville,AL	2:15
Ar. Sheffield. AL	3:00 p.m.

SCHEDULE FOR SUNDAY JANUARY 25, 1981:

Lv. Sheffield, AL	10:30 a.m.
Lv. Iuka, MS	11:30
Lv. Corinth, MS	12:30 p.m.
Lv. Grand Jct., TN	2:00
Lv. Collierville, TN	3:00
Ar. Memphis, TN	4:00 p.m.

This memo is self explanatory. This particular copy was signed by the crew handling the 610 from Sheffield, AL to Memphis, TN and is signed as follows; W. A. Kilgore, road foreman of engines - Bill Purdie, master mechanic - Herman P. Kiser, conductor - C. V. Rudder, engineer - J. E. Barnes, flagman - R. K. Thorne, trainman - J. A. Blasingame, fireman. This copy courtesy of R. K. Thorne.

Memphis and Charleston
RAILROAD.

Local Cotton Tariff,

TO TAKE EFFECT

OCTOBER 1st, 1867,

Between MEMPHIS and the following Stations.

Distances.	Stations.	
9.5	WHITE'S	$ 50
14.5	GERMANTOWN	65
23.8	COLLIERVILLE	80
30.9	LAFAYETTE	1 00
39.0	MOSCOW	1 25
49.0	LAGRANGE,	
52.0	GRAND JUNCTION,	1 50
52.5	SOMERVILLE,	
57.6	SAULSBURY	1 60
69.3	MIDDLETON	1 70
74.4	POCAHONTAS	1 80
83.7	CHEWALLA	1 90
92.8	CORINTH	2 00
107.3	BURNSVILLE,	
114.8	IUKA,	2 10
126.6	DICKSON,	
128.6	CHEROKEE,	2 20
133.3	BARTON,	
145.0	TUSCUMBIA,	
151.0	FLORENCE,	
155.5	LEIGHTON,	
163.0	JONESBORO,	
168.5	COURTLAND,	2 25
176.5	HILLSBORO,	
182.0	TRINITY,	
188.0	DECATUR,	
192.5	MOORESVILLE,	
202.5	MADISON,	
212.0	HUNTSVILLE,	
223.3	BROWNSBORO,	
232.9	PAINT ROCK,	
237.3	WOODVILLE,	2 50
247.7	LARKINSVILLE,	
254.0	SCOTTSBORO,	
259.0	BELLEFONTE,	
271.0	STEVENSON,	
309.0	CHATTANOOGA,	

The following rates of Insurance will be added to the above tariff, unless otherwise ordered by the owner or shipper, which order must be so stated on the receipt given for the Cotton:

From MEMPHIS to GRAND JUNCTION, inclusive, and all Stations intermediate, per Bale, - - 25 cts

" SAULSBURY to CORINTH, inclusive, and all Stations intermediate, per Bale, - - - 30 cts

" BURNSVILLE to DECATUR, inclusive, and all Stations intermediate, per Bale, - - - 40 cts

" DECATUR to CHATTANOOGA, inclusive, and all Stations intermediate, per Bale, - - - 50 cts

The rate from point to point will be ascertained by taking the rate for a similar distance from Memphis.

W. J. ROSS, Gen. Supt.

THOS. B. DUNN, Gen. Freight Agent.

Special Notice to Employees,

MEMPHIS AND CHARLESTON R. R.

Express Trains, Nos. 3 and 4, Time Table No. 22, will meet at Decatur Junction, until further notice.

Express Train No. 3 will leave Decatur	11.25 A. M.
" " arrive Decatur Junc.	11.31 "
" " leave Decatur Junc.	11.36 "
" " No. 4 arrive Decatur Junc.	11.30 "
" " leave Decatur Junc.	11.31 "
" " arrive Decatur	11.38 "

No other change is made in the Time of these Trains. Decatur Junction will be regarded as the meeting point, instead of Decatur as heretofore.

W. J. ROSS, Genl. Supt.

Memphis, Oct. 4th 1868.

Memphis & Charleston R. R.

NOTICE TO EMPLOYEES.

SUPERINTENDENT'S OFFICE,
HUNTSVILLE, ALA., October, 1867.

The following Rules will be observed and continue in force until further notice:

1. Eastward Way Freight, No. 7, will run on Tuesday, Thursday and Saturday.

2. Westward Way Freight, No. 8, will run on Monday, Wednesday and Friday.

3. No. 5 will leave Burnsville at 7:07 P. M., daily, Sundays excepted.

4. No. 6 will leave Huntsville at 7:00 P. M., daily, Saturdays excepted.

5. No. 5 will remain at Burnsville and Huntsville indefinitely, for the arrival of the corresponding train from the West, unless otherwise specially ordered.

6. No. 6 will remain at Stevenson indefinitely, for the arrival of the Freight train from Chattanooga, unless otherwise specially ordered.

7. Conductors of Nos. 5 and 6 will report promptly by telegraph, from Burnsville and Stevenson, giving the number of through cars in their respective trains.

CHARLES S. WILLIAMS,
Assistant Superintendent.

MEMPHIS & CHARLESTON R. R.

(East Tennessee, Virginia and Georgia Railway, Lessee.)

TIME TABLE No. 69.

TO TAKE EFFECT

At 12 o'clock, Noon, Sunday, March 13. 1887.

For the information of employes only—not intended for the public or as an advertisement of the time of trains. The Company reserves the right to vary time of its trains at pleasure.

Trains Run on Central (90th Meridian) Standard Time.

C. H. HUDSON,
General Manager,
Knoxville, Tennessee.

W. R. BEAUPRIE,
Master of Trains.
Tuscumbia, Alabama.

R. B. PEGRAM,
Superintendent,
Memphis, Tennessee.

OGDEN BROS. & CO., PRINTERS & BINDERS.

A 1975 REPRINT BY THE

NORTH ALABAMA RAILROAD CLUB, P.O. BOX 4163, HUNTSVLLE, AL. 35802

WESTERN DIVISION
MEMPHIS AND TUSCUMBIA

2 EASTWARD. (Towards Chattanooga.) — **(From Chattanooga.) WESTWARD 1**

No. 25 Daily P.M. Arrive	No. 23 Daily A.M. Arrive	No. 21 atly. P.M. Arrive	No. 5 Daily Sunday Arrive	No. 3 Daily P.M. Arrive	No. 1 Daily A.M. Arrive	Telegraph Offices	Station Numbers	STATIONS	Distance from Memphis	Capacity Sidings	No. 2 Daily P.M. Leave	No. 4 Daily A.M. Leave	No. 6 Daily ex. Sunday P.M. Arrive
6 00	7 50	11 40	8 30	9 15	6 10	D & N	0	MEMPHIS			10 00	9 30	
5 54	7 41	11 28	8 13	9 11	6 05		2	K.C. Junction	2.0		10 08	9 35	4 41
5 45	7 35	11 21	8 00	9 00	6 02		3	Race Track	3.1	30	10 11	9 39	4 50
5 36	7 23	11 07	7 54	9 05	5 57		5	Buntyn	5.1	30	10 15	9 43	5 05
5 20	7 07	10 53	7 43	8 57	5 50		9	Whites	9.2	58	10 22	9 50	5 20
4 47	6 41	10 33	7 27	8 47	5 38		15	Germantown	11.5	58	10 33	10 02	5 39
4 20	6 13	10 00	7 10	8 35	5 27		20	Bailey	20.3	31	10 45	10 14	6 00
4 00	5 54	9 45	7 00	8 28	5 20	D	24	Collierville	23.9	38	10 52	10 20	6 12
3 28	5 23	9 16	6 40	8 14	5 05	D	31	Rossville	30.9	22	11 06	10 35	6 36
2 50	4 45	8 43	6 15	7 58	4 45	D	39	Moscow	38.0		11 21	10 51	7 05
			5 10			D		Somerville	52.1	38			8 20
2 21	4 06	8 17		7 45	4 36		45	45 Mile Siding	45.2	36	11 34	11 04	
2 04	3 50	8 03		7 38	4 28	D & N	49	Lagrange	48.9	26	11 41	11 11	
1 50	3 37	7 50		7 32	4 22	D	52	Grand Junction	52.0		11 47	11 17	
1 30	3 13	7 21		7 21	4 11		57	Saulsbury	57.2	53	11 58	11 28	
1 01	2 32	6 35		7 05	3 56		61	Sixty-Four	61.0	101	12 12 AM	11 43	
12 27 PM	2 08	6 12		6 55	3 45	D	69	Middleton	69.1	65	12 23	11 53	
11 53	1 42	5 47		6 46	3 34	D		Pocahontas	74.3	34	12 35	12 03 PM	
11 15	1 19	5 25		6 35	3 24	D	79	Cypress	79.0	10	12 45	12 13	
10 45	12 55	5 03		6 27	3 14	D	84	Chewalla	83.7	35	12 55	12 22	
10 20	12 25 AM	4 45		6 20	3 05		87	Wenasoga	87.6	31	1 02	12 30	
9 59	11 52	4 20		6 08	2 53	D	93	Corinth	93.0	57	1 13	12 41	
9 36	11 10	3 41		5 52	2 35		101	Glens	101.0	73	1 30	12 58	
8 50	10 45	3 10		5 48	2 21	D	108	Burnsville	107.7	23	1 43	1 11	
8 05	10 25	2 56		5 35	2 17		109	Walkers Switch	109.3		1 47	1 15	
7 25	9 56	2 26		5 22	2 05	D	115	Iuka	115.2	43	2 05	1 27	
7 10	9 41	2 10		5 16	1 58		118	Gravel Siding	118.4		2 12	1 33	
6 38	9 15	1 44		5 06	1 48		124	Margerum	123.6	19	2 22	1 44	
6 21	8 57	1 15		4 59	1 41		127	Dickson	127.2	33	2 29	1 51	
5 52	8 49	1 05		4 55	1 37		129	Cherokee	129.0	33	2 32	1 55	
5 32	8 25	12 40		4 45	1 28		134	Barton	133.8	33	2 42	2 05	
5 22	8 05	12 15 PM		4 37	1 20		138	Pride	138.0	43	2 50	2 13	
3 50	7 30	11 35		4 22	1 05	D & N	145	TUSCUMBIA	145.4		3 05	2 28	

No. 1 can use full schedule time into Iuka.

No. 3 will take side track at Iuka and wait 5 minutes behind card time for No. 1.

F. figures are in "Italics" except at meeting and passing points.

EASTERN DIVISION.
TUSCUMBIA AND CHATTANOOGA.

EASTWARD. [Towards Chattanooga.] — WESTWARD. [From Chattanooga.]

No.22	No.24	No.26	No.4	No.2	Dist. fr. Memphis	Cap. siding	STATIONS	Sta. No.	Tel.	No.1	No.3	No.25	No.27	No.21
7 20	11 00	4 30	2 35	3 12	145.4		TUSCUMBIA	145	D&N	12 56	4 15	2 40	6 50	10 55
8 11	11 47	5 29	2 57	3 31	155.8	29	Leighton 10.4	156	D	12 37	3 52	1 48	5 45	10 05
8 47	12 21PM	6 12	3 13	3 45	163.1	32	Town Creek 7.3	163		12 22	3 36	1 10	4 58	9 30
9 14	12 46	6 44	3 25	3 55	168.8	30	Courtland 7.7	169	D	12 11	3 25	12 43	4 25	9 04
9 31	1 02	7 05	3 32	4 02	172.4	25	Wheelers 5.6	172		12 05AM	3 12	12 25AM	4 02	8 47
9 49	1 18	7 25	3 40	4 08	176.0	32	Hillsboro 3.6	176	D	11 59	3 03	11 59	3 40	8 30
10 19	1 46	8 00	3 53	4 20	182.2	40	Trinity 6.2	182		11 47	2 50	11 18	2 50	8 00
10 48/11 35	2 15	8 32/9 15	4 07	4 32	188.4		Decatur 6.2	188	D&N	11 35	2 35/2 15	10 48	2 15/1 40	7 26
		9 25	4 14	4 40	190.2	Dec Tank	r Junction 1.8	190	D&N	11 30	2 07	10 39	1 30	7 17
11 43	2 24	9 53	4 25	4 50	196.3	28	Belle Mina 5.1	195		11 20	1 55	10 14	1 03	6 53
12 15	3 00	10 05	4 30	4 55	197.4	21	Greenbrier 2.1	197		11 16	1 50	10 04	12 53	6 44
12 46	3 31	10 36	4 42	5 07	203.2	30	Madison 5.8	203	D	11 04	1 37	9 36	12 22PM	6 17
1 37	4 22	11 30/12 25PM	5 03/5 08	5 27/5 32	212.8	30	Huntsville 9.6	213	D	10 45/10 40	1 15/1 10	8 49	11 30/11 00	5 32
2 00	4 45	1 00	5 17	5 40	217.1	33	Fearns 4.3	217		10 31	1 00	8 28	10 35	4 57
2 37	5 32	1 40	5 32	5 55	224.1	30	Brownsboro 7.0	224	D	10 17	12 45	7 55	9 53	4 26
3 06	6 00	2 10	5 45	6 06	229.5	39	Gurleys 5.4	230	D	10 06	12 32	7 28	9 20	3 52
3 20	6 21	2 34	5 53	6 15	233.7	30	Paint Rock 5.4	234		9 58	12 22	7 09	8 56	3 30
3 50	6 54	3 01	6 03	6 23	238.4	32	Woodville 6.7	238	D	9 48	12 12PM	6 46	8 28	3 00
4 18	7 12	3 36	6 17	6 36	244.6	Tank	Lim Rock 6.2	245	D	9 36	11 57	6 17	7 51	2 32
4 36	7 30	4 00	6 26	6 45	248.7	Tank	Larkinsville 4.1	249	D	9 27	11 48	5 50	7 27	2 15
5 00	7 52	4 30	6 37	6 55	254.1	24	Scottsboro 5.4	254	D	9 16	11 36	5 25	6 55	1 50
5 23	8 15	5 00	6 48	7 05	259.4	54	Ft. Clefonte 3.3	259	D	9 05	11 24	5 00	6 20	1 26
5 50	8 54	5 27	7 00	7 17	265.3	58	Facklers 5.9	265		8 54	11 10	4 30	5 50	1 00
6 20	9 30	6 00	7 15/7 30	7 30/7 45	271.8		STEVENSON N.C.&St.L.R.R. 6.5	272	D&N	8 40	10 55	4 00	5 10	12 30
			9 05	9 15	310.0		CHATTANOOGA	310	D&N	7 10	9 25			

FLORENCE BRANCH.

No.33	No.31	Dist.	Cap.	STATIONS	Tel.No.	Sta.No.	No.32	No.34
4 30	3 15	145.4		TUSCUMBIA 5.4	146	D&N	12 25	2 00
5 30	3 45	150.8		FLORENCE	160	D	11 55	1 10

Between Decatur and Decatur Junction, trains are under control of A.C. Frey, Despatcher, Decatur. East bound trains must not pass Decatur without reporting at Telegraph office. West bound trains can pass Decatur Junction without stopping, when white signal is shown, except when on the time of an East bound train, in which case they must stop for orders.

Between Stevenson and Chattanooga, all trains will be governed by the rules of the Nashville, Chattanooga and St. Louis R. R.

READ THE RULES.
IMPORTANT CHANGES.

7-7-27 20M D. B.

Form 60

SOUTHERN RAILWAY SYSTEM

TELEGRAPHIC REPORT OF BAD ORDER CARS SET OUT SHORT OF DESTINATION

To Train Master
Chief Dispatcher

At ___Sheffield___ Station ___10/27-42___

To Train Master and Chief Dispatcher. "A." Train ___3/31___ "B." 1st Engr. ___C.L.Smith___

"C." 2nd Engr._____ "D." Set off ___Barton___ "G." Intl. ___ATLX___ "H." No ___20224___

"J." Contents ___MT Tank___ "K." From ___240___ "N." Destination ___552___

"Q." Which end is damaged? ___East End___ "R." What is needed to make repairs? If brass state size ___All the Springs & Carry iron cut out___

"S." Way-Bill left at ___Cherokee___ "T." Remarks _____

___W. J. Duncan___ Conductor

Conductors will leave one of these blanks properly filled out with each car set out on account of bad order, short of destination or District Terminal.

Agents will see that the lading of all such cars is protected while at their station and that repairs are made and car moved with least possible delay.

When car goes forward, they should mail this report to Superintendent showing date forwarded.

This report need not be used for Manifest or Time Freight.

This October 27, 1942 form shows that engineer C. L. Smith and conductor W. J. Duncan had to set out a bad order tank car at Barton, AL. Since Barton was not an operator station, the waybill was left at Cherokee. Copy in Jack Daniel Collection.

TELEGRAM

CHIEF DISPATCHER   SHEFFIELD, ALA.
TRAINMASTER   "
GENERAL YARDMASTER   "

_____ 196 _____ 194 2

MAIN 28629 has 2 officers and 51 men with
Lt Burch in charge. Psgr. Agt. None
4:00 PM Departed
No. cars 2 Tonnage 180

E E Stone
Conductor ...

- -

Conductor will fill in and leave at first open telegraph office.
Operator will send quickly as possible--also information on reverse side.
List passenger equipment on back.
Figure tonnage as follows: Coaches 70 tons - Tourist cars 80 tons - Baggage 70
tons - Pullmans 90 tons.

- -

During World War II Southern Railway had many unusual and highly secretive train movements. On October 6, 1942 there was one such move: A two coach train with two Army officers and fifty-one men. Conductor Stone threw this consist report off to the editor at Cherokee, AL to relay to the chief dispatcher in Sheffield, AL but I never learned anymore about the move. These were pprobably some very specialized men that were needed in a hurry somewhere. Copy in Jack Daniel collection.

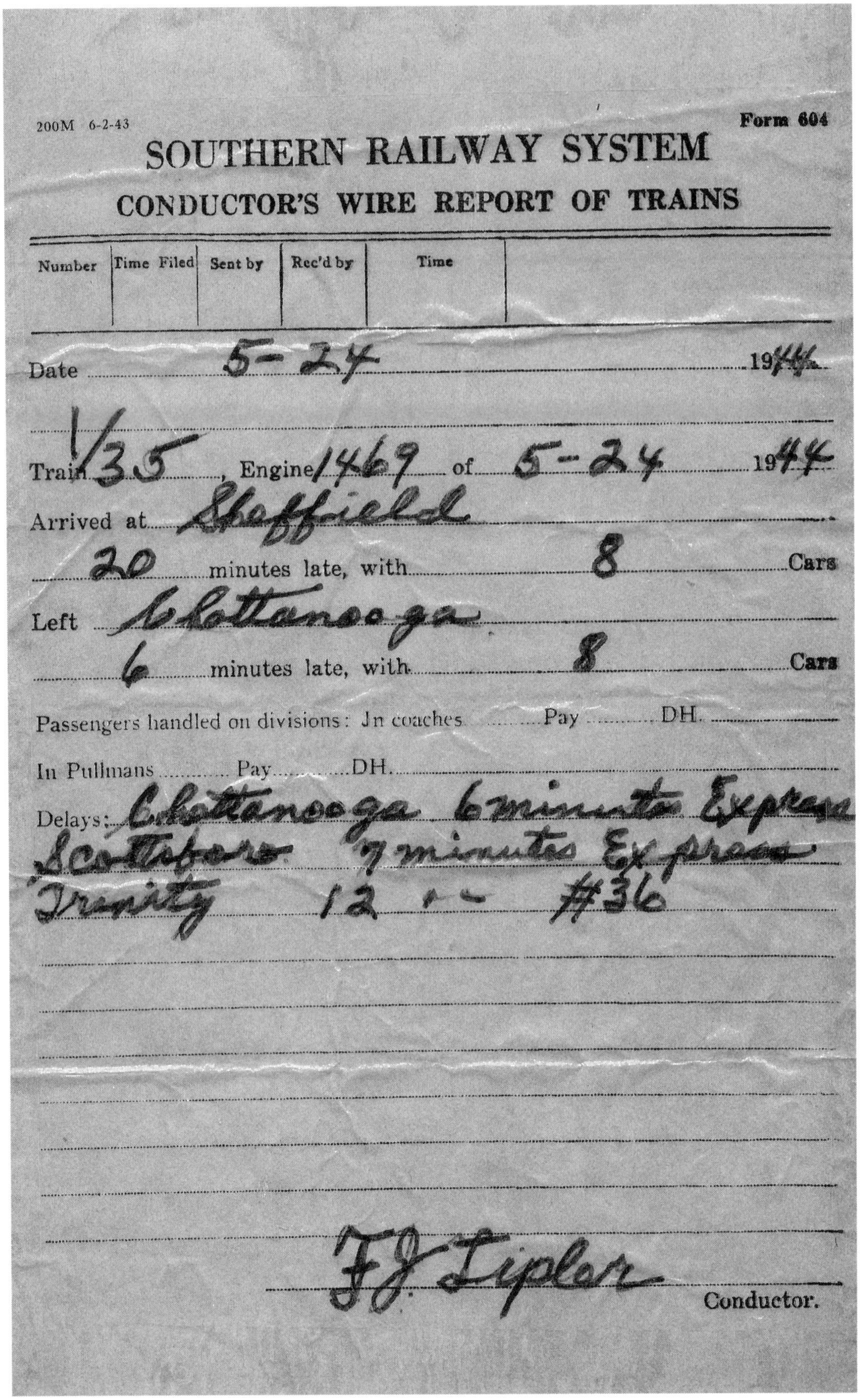

200M 6-2-43

Form 604

SOUTHERN RAILWAY SYSTEM
CONDUCTOR'S WIRE REPORT OF TRAINS

Number	Time Filed	Sent by	Rec'd by	Time	

Date _5-24_ 19_44_

Train _1/35_, Engine _1469_ of _5-24_ 19_44_

Arrived at _Sheffield_

_20_ minutes late, with _8_ Cars

Left _Chattanooga_

_6_ minutes late, with _8_ Cars

Passengers handled on divisions: In coaches _____ Pay _____ DH _____

In Pullmans _____ Pay _____ DH _____

Delays: _Chattanooga 6 minutes Express_
Scottsboro 7 minutes Express
Trinity 12 " - #36

F.J. Tipler
Conductor.

The classes of trains in the steam days were emphasized. Here one can note that only one train delayed first-class train 1st No. 35 this May 24, 1944 and that was another first class train No. 36 who met him at Trinity. No second or third class trains delayed him.

103

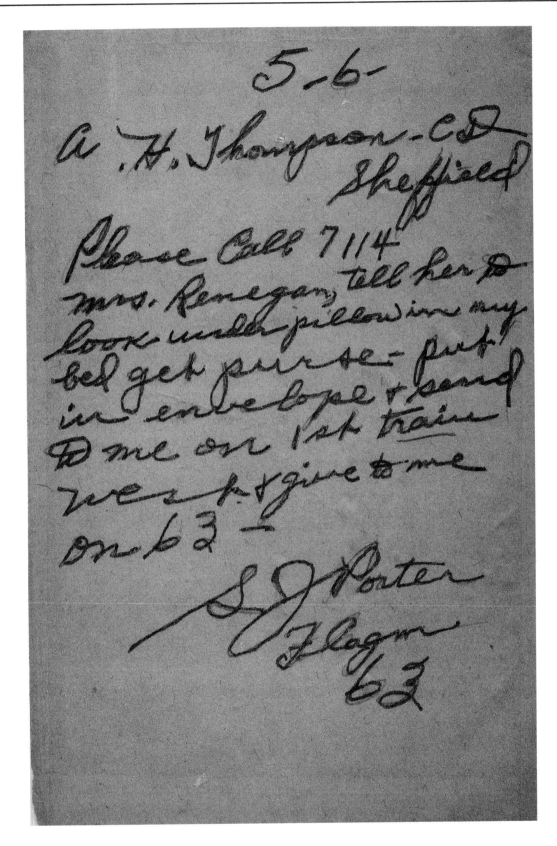

Times haven't changed much when it comes to crew members leaving something on a train that belongs to them. In this case, flagman S. J. Porter, Jr. left his "purse" under his pillow at Mrs. Renegan's boarding house. He probably could have borrowed enough to eat on at Buntyn but he was not taking any chances. S. J. Porter's dad was an engineer and was killed in a headon collision at Glens in 1910.

SOUTHERN RAILWAY COMPANY
CENTRAL LINES
Memphis Division

Sheffield, Ala.- Sept. 5, 1944 vj

BULLETIN
AGENTS, TICKET AGENTS, AGENT OPERATORS AND OPERATORS:

It is noticed that Passenger Conductors are lifting a great number of tickets without dating stamp being shown on the back. You have been instructed in the importance of this and you must not sell any tickets without their being properly stamped with correct date. You should keep your dating stamp with good ribbon so that the impression is legible.

It has also been noticed that some agent Operators and operators have become lax in the observance of passing trains and are not coming out of the office while trains are passing. You must also see that trains are intact when passing your station.

C. D. Vance,
M. J. Bryan,
    Trainmasters

A. H. Thompson
    Chief Dispatcher

*(Bulletins have been and still are a great part of Railroading. Editor.)

Chapter Four

Today's Railroad Men & Machines

Norfolk Southern has 976 locomotives assigned to Chattanoga, Tn.

1	SW1
8	SW1500
33	MP15DC
70	GP38
6	GP38AC
225	GP38-2
4	GP40
3	GP40X
6	GP49
90	GP50
35	GP59
50	GP60
22	SD40
140	SD40-2
6	SD50S
20	SD50
150	SD60
56	SD70
21	B23-7
22	B30-7A
2	RP-E4D
6	RP-E4U

See Note 4

There still is an incredible effort needed to keep the engines of American commerce moving. There are heroes who do their jobs with professionalism and pride, ensuring prompt delivery of goods and safety of crews. They are of the time of the computer, robotic assembly lines, microwave radios and enclosed diesel cabs. Their story is still one of

men and machines

Scenes Along the Line

NS shops at mile post 240-A in Chattanooga, TN.

NS Main Street signal tower in Chattanooga, TN.

Chase Cut at mile post 335-A on Norfolk Southern

Stephens Gap at mile post 309-A on Norfolk Southern

Scottsboro, AL at mile post 298-A was originally called Scott's Mill. The M&C built a water tank here in 1871. The original depot was built in 1861 and survived the Civil War. The first separate passenger depot was built in 1891 at a cost of $1,944.

Stevenson, AL where the Norfolk Southern tracks diverge to the left off of the CSX tracks. Stevenson was the eastern headquarters for the Memphis & Charleston from 1850 until 1898.

A back view of the old Chattanooga, TN depot, now the Chattanooga Choo Choo Hotel.

UP 6799, a rear-end helper on NS coal train 738.

NS ship yard just outside DeButts Yard in Chattanooga, TN.

Old CT Tower at Chattanooga, TN where Tenn. Div. trains used to pick up orders.

Headed west approaching North Tunnel on AGS tracks near Chattanooga, TN.

About to enter North Tunnel on AGS west of Chattanooga, TN.

NS train 226, on left, running around NS coal train Q34 just outside DeButts Yard Chattanooga. 226 engineer G. K. Gooch and conductor J. M. Willis - Q34 engineer P. D. Wright and conductor M. D. Warhurst.

The same 226 as above going under signals at South Tunnel with engineer G. K. Gooch and conductor J. M. Willis.

Entrance to South Tunnel on NS (AGS) tracks.

Stevenson, AL where NS enters CSX tracks to Wauhatchie. Cab & diesel on left parked at Stevenson depot which has been converted to a museum.

Getting off CSX tracks at Wauhatcie and going onto NS (AGS) on right to crossover.

23rd Street Viaduct at Chattanooga, TN.

Headed west approaching Running Water Trestle on CSX tracks Whiteside, TN.

Running Water Trestle crossing over interstate highway at Whiteside, TN.

Drawbridge at Bridgeport, AL on CSX tracks. NS has trackage rights.

Beginning removal of old track over Tennessee River bridge at Bridgeport, AL. This section of new track has concrete ties. NS has trackage rights with CSX from Stevenson, AL to Chattanooga, TN.

CSX double track at Whiteside, TN where NS has trackage rights from Wauhatchie to Stevenson, AL.

North end of NS Drawbridge at Decatur, AL

Approaching from the east to Wheeler, AL. Signal is red for a meet.

Approaching east end of Sheffield, AL yards. First track to left is Chattanooga outbound track.

Norfolk Southern's Receiving Yard at Sheffield, AL, opened sometime in 1974.

Norfolk Southern's Master Retarder in Class Yard at Sheffield, AL.

Norfolk Southern's Class Yard at Sheffield, AL, opened sometime in 1974.

Norfolk Southern's Diesel Shop at Sheffield, AL.

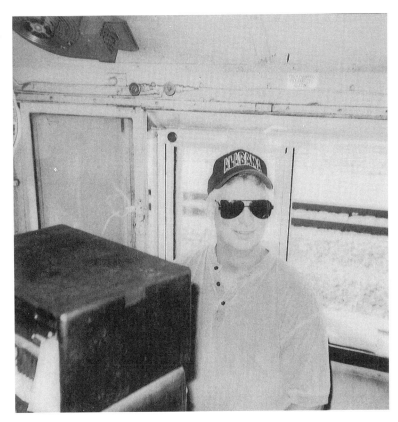

Steve Collingsworth, NS engineer (entered service 2-26-80) working the "Pull-back" at Sheffield, AL Yards. Steve's dad was General Shop Foreman for Southern. Photo courtesy of Debra Bacon, Muscle Shoals, AL.

Mr. Jim B. Painter, NS Superintendent of Terminals at Sheffield, AL (entered service August 29, 1964), decorates his office with his switch key collection. He has collected 57 keys with the oldest being over 100 years and is from the Memphis & Charleston Railroad. Jim is currently out of service with blood pressure problems. Photo in Jack Daniel collection.

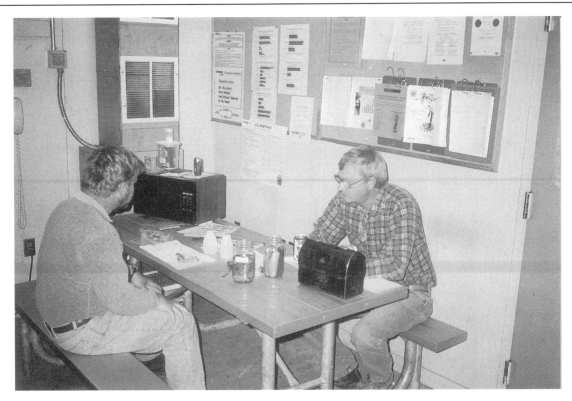

Left; J. E. Walker, NS Engineer at Sheffield, AL Yard. Entered service November 1, 1985. Right; J. H. Pace, NS Switchman at Sheffield, AL Yard. Entered service February 4, 1971.

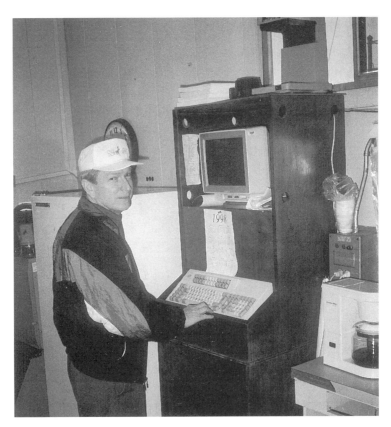

Truman Kimbrough, Norfolk Southern Hump Foreman at Sheffield, AL Yard. Entered service April 28, 1969.

Jim Spencer, Norfolk Southern Inbound Clerk at Sheffield AL Yards.

Victor Ashby, Norfolk Southern Outbound Clerk at Sheffield, AL Yards.

124

L. T. Kimbrough, Norfolk Southern Yard Foreman at Sheffield AL Yards Hump. Entered service April 28, 1979.

Randy Mansell, Norfolk Southern Yardmaster at Sheffield, AL Yards. Entered service October 27, 1978.

J. P. Fuller, Norfolk Southern Yard Switchman at Sheffield AL Yards Hump. Entered service June 11, 1977.

L. D. Dalrymple, Norfolk Southern Switchman at Sheffield, AL Yards Hump. Entered service March 2, 1970.

Norfolk Southern's Sheffield, AL yard has been the recipient of the E. H. Harriman Safety Award for a number of years as per the sign at the entrance to the yard.

The Safety Building on the NS Sheffield, AL property.

The new Norfolk Southern Sheffield, AL yard has experienced one accidental death of an employee since its opening in 1974. This Memorial is to Jerry H. Scott, an engineer. The inscription reads; *"An unforgettable friend whose humor, loyalty and self dedicated service, left us all a lasting inspiration."* The Sheffield Safety Building is in the foreground.

128

NS classification yard at Sheffield, AL.

6th Street crossing before entering east end of Double track running to Tuscumbia, AL.

The old Tuscumbia, AL 5th Street passenger station which was built by the Memphis & Charleston Railroad on October 16, 1888, was also used by the Southern Railway. The upper story was used as M&C administrative offices. The building now serves as the Tuscumbia Senior Center. The carport was added later. Photo courtesy of Rayburn Pace.

What was once the mainline of the Memphis & Charleston Railroad, that ran up the middle of 5th Street in Tuscumbia, AL eastward to Stevenson, AL, used to bypass Sheffield. The old track now deadends at the old Tuscumbia, AL 5th Street depot. An ex-Southern Railway caboose is now displayed with an advertisement of the original Tuscumbia Railway which was about three and one half miles long and was in existence from 1830 till 1832. This railroad used horses for power to pull one coach that resembled a stage coach. Photo courtesy of Rayburn Pace.

West end of double track at Tuscumbia, AL heading west to Memphis, TN.

Train 362-T7 at Pride, AL-Engineer Ty Thompson & conductor J. C. "Killer" Kilpatrick 8-26-97 - Track on right leads to the TVA Colbert Steam Plant .

Train 364 T7 taking siding at Oldham, MS with NS engineer H. R. Patterson and NS conductor L. E. Grisham - 8-24-97

NS bridge over the Tennessee-Tombigbee Canal at Burnsville, MS.

Interlocking with Kansas City Southern Railroad at Corinth, MS.

NS engineer P. D. Wright on train 777 T7 engine 9096 at Rossville, TN.

NS conductor Mike D. "Mad Dog" Warhurst on train 777 T7 Rossville, TN.

NS engineer Charlie Beckwith & NS conductor J. Cliff Wade taking siding Rossville,
TN with Union Pacific engine 6297.

NS conductor Mike D. Warhurst lining up behind train in previous picture.

On left, NS engineer P. D. Wright and on right, NS conductor Mike Warhurst have a great smile at end of a trip. Book men are good natured and friendly. Photo by Jack Daniel.

1

Southern Rwy. train # 88 with engine 2621 in summer of 1979 with engineer Bill "Willie D." Hutton, conductor B. J. Malone, brakeman Andy Posey and flagman Bobby Lewis made it to Collierville and the crossing near Alpha Chemical when a concrete mixing truck pulled out in front of train. The engine was running long-hood forward and the impact tore the concrete truck all to pieces. Driver of truck was killed.

2

The concrete mixing cylinder was broken apart and the concrete flew back and splattered all over the south side of the locomotive. All the windows and windshield were broken out of this side. Andy Posey fell to the floor which probably saved his life.

3

This is what remained of the concrete truck. A westbound train waiting at Rossville came and pulled No. 88 to Rossville and 88's crew was relieved of duty for the rest of the trip.

NS stack train # 286 with UP engines 9027 and 4206 approaching Germantown, TN at mile post 537.2 on August 9, 1997 with engineer Randy G. Malone. Randy entered service on April 11, 1980. I did not see who the conductor was. Photo by Jack Daniel.

Norfolk Southern stack train on the NA at Bear Creek, Alabama.

NS conductor James Bennett boards NS GP38-AC No. 4144 at mile post 432 Oldham, MS westbound 8-14-97. Photo by Barry Boothe, Iuka, MS

NS Dash 940 CW # 8926 at mile post 432.2 eastbound, experiencing broken air hose on 3-17-97. Photo by Barry Boothe, Iuka, MS.

NS Dash 9-41C # 9126 and SD 60 # 6683 passes under Natchex Trace m.p. 425 eastbound 6-11-97 Photo by Barry Boothe, Iuka, MS.

NS SD40-2 # 6133 and 6122 at Carlin m.p. 414 west of Tuscumbia, AL on 7-1-97. Photo by Barry Boothe.

NS Dash 9-40C # 8797 and SD 70 # 2513 with empty coal train at Carlin m.p. 414 in April, 1996. Photo by Barry Boothe, Iuka, MS.

NS SD70 # 2508 moving fast at m.p. 432.2 with pig train 4-8-97. Photo by Barry Boothe.

NS SD40-2 # 3320 at m.p. 431.5 on 8-14-97. Photo by Barry Boothe, Iuka, MS.

NS Dash 9-40C # 8877 leads C36-7 # 8505 in Iuka, MS in July, 1996. Photo by Barry Boothe.

NS SW1500 # 2330 in Sheffield, AL yard 2-22-96. Engineer Brad E. Riley. Photo by Barry Boothe, Iuka, MS.

UP Dash 8-41CW # 9497 and NS Dash 9 # 8869 at Oldham, MS 11-25-96. 1996. Photo by Barry Boothe.

Cotton Belt GP60 # 9696 meets UP AC4400CW # 6887 at Oldham, MS 4-18-97. Photo by Barry Boothe, Iuka, MS.

SP B30-7 # 7850 at m.p. 414.2 Pride, AL 4-25-97. 1996. Photo by Barry Boothe.

SP SD40T-2 # 8531 at m.p. 432 in August, 1997. Believed to be tunnel motor. Photo by Barry Boothe, Iuka, MS.

SP AC4400CW # 195 at Iuka, MS 3-17-97. Photo by Barry Boothe.

Cotton Belt GP60 # 9696 & UP SD40-2B # 3132 & SP GP60 # 9734 at m.p. 431.9 on 4-18-97. Photo by Barry Boothe.

Santa Fe 8-40CW # 802 and 875 with stack train at m.p. 415.4 near Colbert Steam Plant on 5-3-97. Photo by Barry Boothe.

Canadian National SD40 # 5928 near Pride, AL Barn in background is on NS conductor Ricky Moultrie's farm. Photo by Barry Boothe.

Southern X412 in fresh paint near Vertagreen turnout at Cherokee, AL in 1997. Photo by Barry Boothe.

146

Southern Railway # 1486, a Ts Mountain type locomotive with a 4-8-2 wheel arrangement was built by Baldwin in 1917. These beautiful engines served Southern for about 36 years in passenger service. Some of them were used in freight and yard service after their retirement and before they were scrapped. The editor thinks these engines were the most beautiful and balanced looking engines on the system. Photo in editor's collection.

Locomotive 4610 was painted in Southern Railway colors at the Chattanooga, TN shops. The occasion was to celebrate the centennial anniversary of the Southern. Norfolk Southern sends the engine all over the system for employees and the public to see. Photo courtesy of "Conductor Dave" Jordan.

148

CNW SD40-2 # 6902 painted in "Operation Lifesaver" logo was photographed May 4, 1996 at Pride, AL on an eastbound Norfolk Southern coal train. Photo courtesy of Barry Boothe.

Norfolk Southern GP59 # 4630 with "Operation Lifesaver" logo is photographed at about the same location as the one one the preceding page which is Pride, AL on April 25, 1997. The Sheffield to Cherokee turn-around has local dignitaries and local law enforcement officers on board. A cab mounted camera showed the passengers what the engineer saw via a monitor in the passenger car. This was a dramatic way of showing local people the dangers of trying to "beat the train." Photo by Barry Boothe, 133 County Road 255, Iuka, MS 38852.

Norfolk Southern engineer G. Kenny Gooch (entered service 10-31-88). Photo courtesy T. R. Wagnon

Paul D. Pate (employed 8-4-78) as a brakeman. Photo courtesy T. R. Wagnon.

Mike Q. Malone, NS engineer (entered service 7-26-94) and Lewis Acklin, NS conductor (entered service 12-28-87) on NS engine 7141, a GP60, as a work train for unloading riprapping rock. Pictured here at Oldham, MS, in July, 1996. Photo by Barry Boothe, 133 County Road 255, Iuka, MS 38852.

Brad E. Riley, NS engineer (entered service 2-1-77) on SW1500 # 2330 at Sheffield, AL tie yard. Photo by Barry Boothe.

NS engineer Raymond Gene Elliott (entered service 3-14-73) on SP 8256 at Oldham, MS. Photo by Barry Boothe, 133 County Road 255, Iuka, MS 38852

NS engineer Ty Thompson (entered service 5-20-94) on SP 9610 at Pride, AL. Photo by Barry Boothe, 133 County Road 255, Iuka, MS 38852

" The 100 Year Crew"

L to R; **Brad Eugene Riley**, NS engineer - **C. W. "Buzz" Malone**, NS switchman and **N. A. "Abe" Vandiver**, NS switchman standing in front of GP38-2 number 5108 at the Sheffield Alabama Tie Yard on November 26, 1997. Photo by Barry Boothe.

The combined total years of service of this crew is 100 years. Brad Riley has 30 years, Buzz Malone has 32 years and Abe Vandiver has 38 years, at the time of the photo. This crew made history when they were the crew that made the last run across the Florence bridge. It was history because the bridge had been used for railroad service for 146 years. The engine 1010 that they were on that day is long gone as it was traded in to the Electro Motive Division of GM on February 23, 1977. It was an SW-1 type engine with 600 h.p. with a 600 gallon fuel capacity, 125 gallons of water and 28 cubit feet sand capacity.

However, the 5108 pictured above, a GP38-2 type would never been allowed to cross the bridge because of the weight. It was built in January of 1974 and has 2,000 h.p., 2,600 gallon fuel capacity, 240 gallons of water and 72 cubit feet sand capacity.

Norfolk Southern abandoned the old Florence Bridge in 1986. The bridge had a long and eventful history. The first bridge was a wooden structure built in 1840 for horse and wagon and cattle traffic. In 1853, two spans were were blown away by a tornado and it was out of service until 1857 when the Memphis & Charleston Railroad rebuilt it for both wagon and train traffic. M&C's chief engineer gave a very detailed report of the cost of the bridge in 1861 as follows; grading $25,570 - masonry work $51,617 - bridge superstructure and trestles $69,729 - rails, spikes and frogs $29,914 - crossties, track laying and ditching $6,631 - land damages and depot ground $1,270 - toll bridge franchise $23,000 - engineering $3,838 - Grand total $217, 596.

On the morning of April 4, 1860 this bridge was struck by a tornado and 1,050 feet of the roof, or where the tracks were, was torn away. Crews made repairs and had traffic flowing by December, 1860. Then in 1862 during the Civil War, the bridge was burned by the yankees. It was not rebuilt until 1870 and was out of service the eight years.

A TIME CAPSULE OF THE FLORENCE BRIDGE

1840	first wooden bridge built for wagon and cattle traffic by Territorial government.
1853	two spans destroyed by tornado and out of service until 1857.
1856-57	Memphis & Charleston Railroad purchases and rebuilds for both wagon and train traffic.
1860	1,050 feet of top destroyed by tornado. quickly repaired.
1862	yankees burned it during Civil War. Not rebuilt until 1870.
1891	north end approach fell when L&N ore train crossed. Engine stayed on tracks.
1892	locomotive and 6 cars fall through including engineer Clam, fireman Hamlet. No one killed. 150 foot span fell. Bridge condemned.
1896	discontent over the M&C bridge tolls severe enough that Florence businessmen announced a boycott.
1899	Southern Railway forced by courts to lower tolls across bridge. Rates were as follows - each person 10 cents - horses, mules, cattle in droves 7 cents each - one man and one horse 15 cents - one horse and one buggy 20 cents - special school tickets 3 cents.
1904	Street cars or trolleys allowed to use bridge.
1962	old turn-span replaced by a lift-span.
1986	Norfolk Southern Railroad abandons bridge.
1990	Old Railroad Bridge Company formed and received deed to bridge from Norfolk Southern. This organization dedicated to preserving it for a pedestrian and bicycle trail. Norfolk Southern donates $250,000 to the ORBC to be used in the restoration.
1992	old lift span removed and moved by barge to Hannibal, Missouri to be used at another river crossing.

Norfolk Southern Employees

Memphis District

Most Poplar First Name of Train Crews

Steve
1. Steve Phillips — Engineer
2. Steve Davidson — Engineer
3. Steve Hudson — Engineer
4. Steve Rhodes — Engineer
5. Steve Anderson — Engineer
6. Steve Collingsworth — Engineer
7. Steve Southern — Conductor
8. Steve Pickering — Conductor
9. Steve Pope — Conductor

Mike
1. Mike Quillen — Engineer
2. Mike Hill — Engineer
3. Mike Malone — Engineer
4. Mike Myhan — Engineer
5. Mike Worsham — Engineer
6. Mike Jackson — Conductor
7. Mike Warhurst — Conductor
8. Mike Bishop — Conductor
9. Mike Goodman — Conductor
10. Mike Berry — Brakeman
11. Mike Cook — Brakeman

Phillip
1. Phillip Crowe — Engineer
2. Phillip Murphy — Engineer
3. Phillip Wright — Engineer
4. Phillip Kirk — Engineer
5. Phillip Diremeyer — Conductor
6. Phillip Bates — Brakeman
7. Phillip Brewer — Conductor trainee

There were several new trainees that were hired in late 1998 that will have their names on seniority list but do not have pictures in book.

A Special Thanks to

Melvyn Ray Myhan - Norfolk Southern conductor

The editor would like to especially thank Melvyn for an enormous contribution to the book. Over a period of time, he collected several photographs that he used to help him recognize and better identify fellow workers and we appreciate his sharing them for the book.

Melvyn grew up with the railroad. He lived just three blocks from the railroad tracks that passed behind Village One in Sheffield, Alabama. He woke up many mornings with a train whistle as his alarm clock. Melvyn entered service of the Southern Railway in 1968, not moving into a regular job until 1969 when he went to work as conductor in the Decatur, AL Yards. He remained in Decatur for the next fifteen years before deciding to "spread wings" and go on the road. He has worked the Scottsboro turn, Jackson turn, Corinth local and the extra board. He has worked the Memphis to Chattanooga, TN runs including work trains. Each job has had new people and experiences for Melvyn, which he considers important.

Melvyn married Donna Box and she is employed as Colbert County Administrator with offices in the Colbert County Courthouse in Tuscumbia, AL. Melvyn and Donna have five children: Steven Wade, Shannon Ray, Stacy Leigh, Amanda Nicole and Richard Chad. They also have two wonderful grand-daughters named Lauren Jackson and Mary Caitlin.

A Special Thanks to

Mike D. Warhurst - Norfolk Southern conductor

l to r: Rhonda, Conner, and Mike Warhurst. "Chancy" the dog is posing also. The second dog "Risky" was not interested. Mike entered service of the Southern Railway on August 3, 1979. Little Conner should make a railroader by the year 2023. Mike attended schools in Cherokee and Muscle Shoals, AL and presently lives in Muscle Shoals.

P. D. Wright - Norfolk Southern engineer

Phillip D. Wright entered service of the Southern Railway on October 20, 1979 and is pictured here with wife Sandra and sons Joseph and Jacob. Phillip is the only person the editor ever knew that was married in a wheel chair. He broke his leg and dislocated a shoulder a week before his wedding date. He couldn't walk due to the broken leg and couldn't use crutches because of his shoulder, so they pushed him down the aisle in a wheel chair. Later, P. D. was off work for five months to have his shoulder operated on. How's that for determination?

158

A Special Thanks to

Tim W. Wagnon - Norfolk Southern engineer

Tim entered service of the Southern Railway on July 17, 1981. He and wife Cindy have a daughter named April and a son named Adam. The editor used to work with many of his Aunts and Uncles.

T. David Jordan - Norfolk Southern conductor

Dave, better known as "Conductor Dave" entered service of the Southern Railway on July 16, 1972. He and wife Marilyn have one son, Kevin David Jordan. Dave currently lives in Russellville, Alabama.

A Special Thanks to

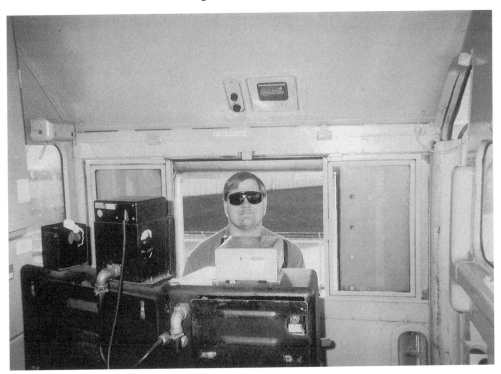

Lance Underwood - Norfolk Southern engineer

Lance entered service of the Southern Railway on April 9, 1976. Lance made contributions to the book representing the Decatur, Alabama area. Lance and his parents are longtime friends of the editor.

Rayburn Pace - Norfolk Southern hump foreman

Rayburn entered service of the Southern Railway on May 7, 1971. He and wife Thelma have two sons, Gregory and Darrell. Rayburn and Thelma are restoring a beautiful home near Leighton, Alabama.

A Special Thank You to

J. R. "Bobby" Balentine - Norfolk Southern engineer

Bobby entered service of the Norfolk Southern Railroad on November 1, 1988. He is presently assigned to the old Northern Alabama district of the Alabama Division that runs from Sheffield to Birmingham, AL. Bobby was helpful and made contributions to the book from the NA. Bobby and wife Rhonda have a daughter, Jennifer Balentine Fuller and a son, Brad with one granddaughter, Leslie Fuller. The editor graduated high school in Cherokee, Alabama with Bobby's mother, Dorothy Maxwell.

Bill "Willie D." Hutton - Norfolk Southern engineer

Bill entered service of Southern Rwy. on March 14, 1973. He is one of seven brothers and sisters who were born near Pulaski, TN. He received his nickname "Willie D." from Crawford Barnes, a retired Southern Railway engineer who recently died 1-10-99. Bill lives on County Line Road near Leighton, AL with wife, Vickie. He enjoys horseback riding and hunting elk in Colorado where he and several friends go each year. Bill made contributions to the book.

Left- Engineer Phillip W. Crowe (Entered service 10-21-80)- Right-Conductor Dave Jordan (Entered service 7-16-72)

****

Conductor Dave Jordan
Russellville, Alabama 35653

Jack Daniel
3467 Alfred Drive
Memphis, TN 38133

Hello Jack:

    I have often wondered how much the railroad has really changed in the last twenty-seven years or should it be how much have I changed? I began my career for the Southern Railway in the early seventies. I think I have heard all the stories of steam railroading more than once. When I went to work most of the older people began their careers during World

War II. I learned that these older railroaders loved to tell their favorite stories. I was young and I was interested in their stories to a certain extent but I heard them enough to have them memorized. I did learn from these stories, however, that there was a lot of self pride and tradition in working for the railroad. I think I have some in me.

In the old days everyone was exposed to the elements of the weather. The cabs of the steam engines were open and therefore they were hot in the summer and cold in the winter. The days were long, hard, and consecutive. There were not many days off. These conditions caused these men to spend a lot of time together, and they spent more time with each other than they did with their families. This happened to me to some extent. I was young as were the rest of the men that went to work when I did. We sort of grew up together, living in dormitories and working long hours together.

How times have changed. The first big change came with the diesel electric engines with enclosed cabs. A lot of these older diesels were still around when I went to work. The railroad would just keep rebuilding them by robbing parts off another to keep as many running as they could. There were a few new engines on our division, but they were only used on the hotshots, the good jobs. A lot of those hotshot trains had nicknames like "The Dixie Belle," and "Roadrunner," plus a few other. Railroaders loved to put names on the trains and nicknames for their buddies too. Some of the nicknames that come to mind are "Buttermilk," "Jug," "Nubbin," "Hand Can," "Tatter," "Flat Wheels." All these nicknames had a story behind them as to how they came about. The tradition continues today as we have our own stories and nicknames.

Enclosed cabs were a big change, but there were more to come. We lost a lot of co-workers. With better communications the railroad closed depots and cut the number of employees. Clerk positions were cut and train crew size was reduced. While the loss of jobs was important, I don't think it was a controlling factor that made the difference between then and now.

The new locomotives, the big ones, separated us from the past. The new engines have computers, air conditioning, soft floors, sound proofing, ultra violet shields in the glass, and many more improvements. We sit up high on the rails traveling up and down better tracks with our microwave radio telephones that has revolutionized railroading.

Jack, as you know, I met you a few years ago but it seems like we have been friends all my life. It is nice that we share a common interest in railroading and we know a lot of the same people. I want to thank you for reminding me, through your book *Southern Railway:Stevenson to Memphis*, that there is pride in our working for the railroad and I could close my eyes and smell the scent of new cross ties. I am looking forward to your new book combining the old and the new. It was nice to reminisce about the guys I knew a few years ago. Today we have new stories to tell. You know, we still talk about good times, laugh about embarrassing situations, and agonize over the problems of today's railroading. Comaraderie still exists today. We are proud to continue to serve this little corner of the south and be a part of the "Thoroughbreds of Railroading" and we enjoy seeing our area grow economically.

Happy Railroading,

Conductor Dave

P. D. Wright - engineer

Bill "Willie D" Hutton - engineer

These four railroaders are representative of the "Thoroughbreds of Railroading" of the Norfolk Southern Railroad's Memphis & NA Districts. These "Thoroughbreds" started out "Serving the South" for the Southern Railway . They saw the system grow into the merged Norfolk Southern. They witnessed the transition of first generation diesels to today's larger horsepowered engines. If they have a home computer, they can check how many "times out" they are. They see much improved roadbeds, track and bridges. They are handling much heavier trains today which requires more powerful locomotives. They see more foreign power on the road with many "run-through" trains. They handle trains of diverse commodities, including solid unit-trains of coal, wheat, sulphur and many other items that were not handled in this area a few years ago. Their locomotives have on-board computers, heating and air conditioning , noise reduction, microwave radios, that work most of the time, plus many other improvements. Today's railroader can get the current temperature at hotbox detectors that are located about every fifteen miles along the line.

Current day railroaders have a lot to be thankful for and most of them realize this. They still agonize over problems that beset their duties . They see that sometimes it still takes too long to complete a run. Frustrations have always been around with any generation of railroader. They, like railroaders before them, have hope that the planners and implementors will continue to work for better and improved railroading and working conditions. After the beginner gets off the extra board and gets a few "whiskers," railroaders begin to be paid a modest income. Just as their predecessors, they generally like their job in spite of the time away from home but they still look forward to those much earned vacations.

WE SALUTE ALL RAILROADERS OF THE MEMPHIS & N.A. DISTRICTS OF NORFOLK SOUTHERN RAILROAD FOR CONTINUING THE TRADITION OF "STEEL WHEELS ON STEEL RAILS."   LET'S KEEP HAVING A SAFE TRIP !

Jack Daniel

J. C. Kilpatrick - conductor

Mike D. Warhurst - conductor

164

Norfolk Southern Employees on the N. A. (Northern Alabama)

This is a photo of Northern Alabama Railroad caboose No. 601 with old archbar trucks at Littleville, Alabama. Conductor J. W. Christian is in the doorway and the engineer, fireman, brakeman and flagman also pose for the photo. Mr. Christian entered service on August 19, 1923, so I would speculate that this photo was made sometime in the middle of the late 1920s. Photo in Jack Daniel collection.

Parrish, Alabama was named for a Mr. Parrish who came from England and bought land in and around where Parrish is today. He no doubt was speculating on the coal reserves in that area. He also bought land in and around Riverton, Alabama. Riverton was beginning to be established. Parrish planned to build a railroad from Parrish to Sheffield, Alabama and then get trackage rights from the Memphis & Charleston Railroad westward to Margerum, AL, thence branch off and go northward to the newly planned Riverton. The Birmingham, Sheffield and Tennessee Railroad was given a charter and later became the Northern Alabama Railroad. This line was later absorbed into the Southern Railway System as the Northern Alabama Division. This road is in the Alabama Division of the Norfolk Southern Railroad today and is still referred to as the "N.A." The old branch line to Riverton was abandoned in the early 1900s.

Left: Robert ("Daddy-O") Williams - conductor (entered service 2-13-70)
Right: Hugh ("Paw Paw") Garrett - conductor (entered service 2-3-69)

166

Johnny Badgett - engineer (entered service 4-1-70)

Jimmy Dolan - conductor (entered service 7-6-77)

When NA crews deadhead, they often stop at this BP station in Cullman, AL for coffee.

David Hall - conductor (entered service 9-1-78)

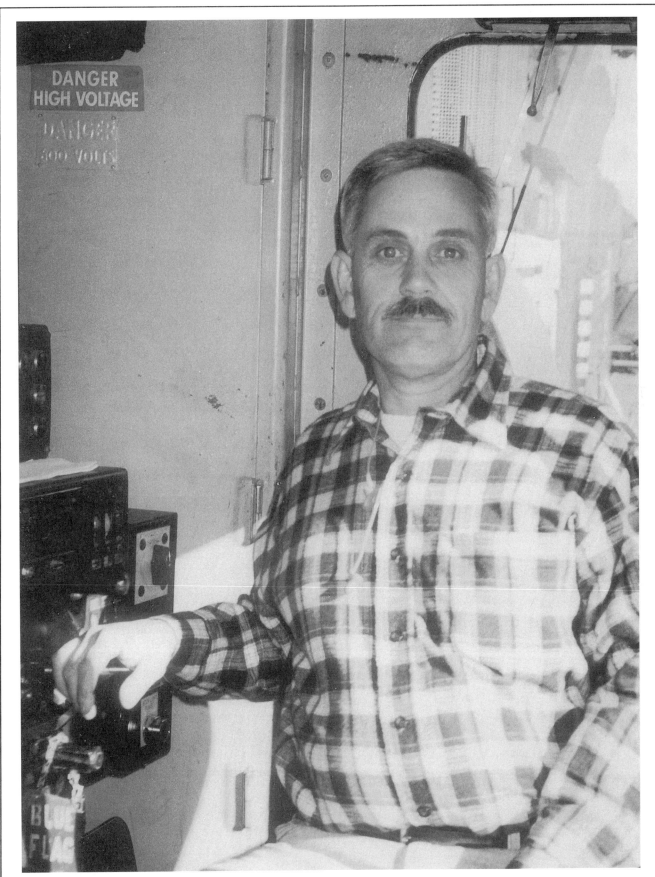

Tommy ("Knucklepin") Beard, conductor (entered service 3-5-79) is also qualified as an engineer when needed.

Left: Clyde Sizemore - brakeman (entered service 4-12-70)
Center: J. D. Dotson - conductor (entered service 2-20-70)
Right: Dave Thornton - engineer (entered service 11-1-70)
The A76 local crew from Sheffield to Haleyville, AL and back on Monday through Friday.

Left: Donnie Daugherty - conductor (entered service 12-7-79)
Center: Eddie Ramsey - conductor (entered service 11-16-78)
Right: Danny Weeks - engineer (entered service 8-12-80)

Shorty Jones - conductor (entered service 2-1-74)

**Left: Robert ("Daddy-O") Williams - conductor (entered service 2-13-70)
Right: Danny Pickett - engineer (entered service 7-1-90)**

John King - conductor (entered service 3-5-79)

Jimmy ("Peanut") Askew entered service as a brakeman in March of 1968 and his seniority date as engineer began November of 1970.

NS engineer Jimmy ("Peanut") Askew entered service as a brakeman in March of 1968 and and his seniority date as engineer began in November of 1970. Pictured here in February, 1999 on locomotive 9047, southbound on the NA. Jimmy was named for his greatuncle, J. T. Askew, who was a conductor on the Southern Railway. Mr. Jim was born in Cherokee, Alabama.

On the trip with Jimmy Askew is conductor John King whose seniority date is March 5, 1979.

174

NS 9047 in siding at
Gamble, AL on the NA
waiting on meet.
Conductor John King
is on ground

Northbound *NS* 7013
meets the 9047 at
Gamble, AL in
February, 1999.

Rearend of *NS* 7013
passes with EOT
device working well.

NS conductor Ron Eudy who entered service on September 16, 1972.

NS conductor Tommy Sharp who entered service January 4, 1972.

NS yard and siding at Parrish, AL on the NA.

NS "wye" at Parrish, AL on NA. Track to left goes to coal mines.

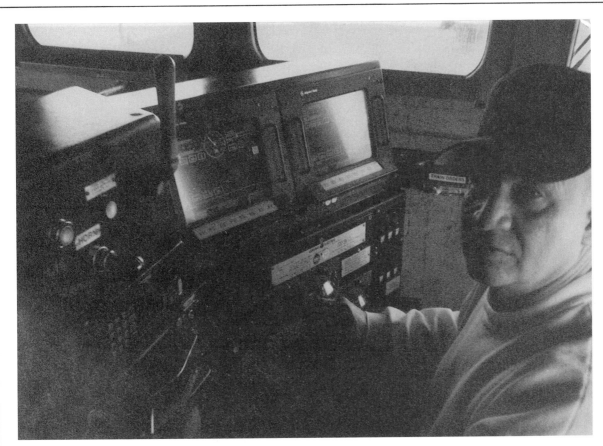

Pictured here is *NS* engineer Jimmy Askew inside the cab of locomotive *NS* 9047. The 9047 is one of 354 GE Dash 9-40CW locomotives that *NS* owns. This unit was delivered for service on February 20, 1997. It has a CC 7FDL16 engine; 83:20 gear ratio; 4,000 horsepower; 410,000 pounds operating weight. It is equipped with IFC or CCB2 electronic air brakes. The horn is in the center of the top of the engine and the bell is attached to the fuel tank. This makes for a more noise-free cab. One other great improvement is the microwave radios that allow for communications between crews, dispatchers, and yardmasters. The age of the computer is being utilized by the railroads as you can see the computer screens in the picture above.

These locomotives are truly a greatly advanced piece of machinery but this is only the beginning. Greater improvements have already been made on a later model than the 9-40CW and even greater improvements are on the drawing board.

The employees that ride these giants are a special breed too. They are dedicated to their work and always have safety-first in their minds. Their fellowship and comradery makes for one great family.

178

Pete Futrell - NA conductor for *NS* (Seniority date 9-17-72)

Charlie Garner - NA conductor for *NS* - (seniority date 3-26-76) in cab of *NS* 9186

Southern Railway 6108, first F-3 diesel on the Memphis Division. L to R; J. H. Ray Bishop, head brakeman - Russell Morgan, fireman - Willard Brown, traveling electrician - Ralph Cutler, engineer - Charles L. Smith, road foreman of engines. Photo in Jack Daniel collection.

A Railroad Can Run Better With Pride and Attitude

Most all railroad men love their work and take *pride* in it, even though a few of them will not admit it. Most of them exhibit a corporate loyalty and are careful to protect their employer's interest. A goodly part of their satisfaction arises from the belief that the job they perform is worthwhile and necessary and contributes to the growth of the United States economy.

I recognized and witnessed all of the above situations in the men who railroaded during the Southern Railway System days. They had much *pride* and good *attitudes* as they "Served the South."

A railroad scanner is a wonderous piece of equipment for me. The scanner can be a window into the soul of a railroad. Listening to a scanner most of the day can tell one what railroaders really think about their jobs.

I have heard some comments from the employees on the Memphis District of the Norfolk Southern Railroad that make me realize that these "modern day" railroaders have as much *pride* and good *attitudes* as any railroader at any time. Among some of the better comments I have heard;

(1) "If the trains didn't run, the customers aren't served and nobody gets paid." (2)"Yeah, sometimes people forget that the whole idea is to run trains and serve the customers." (3)"I'm out here trying to serve the South." (4)"I have kept a record of all my trips ever since I began railroading."

Let me close these comments by telling you about a proposal that is being tested that places horns on crossing signals that will sound a warning instead of the engineer having to blow the warning himself. The horns will be mounted on the signal stands and a strobe light will let the engineer know the horns are working. Since the stationary horns will direct the sound toward roadway traffic, they will lower the decibel levels and thereby reduce noise to the nearby residents. I would believe that this practice would be limited to those crossings that have a large amount of road traffic in larger towns and cities. I don't know about you but I kinda like the engineer blowing the horn as they always have. *Jack Daniel - editor*

<u>Norfolk Southern Employees - Memphis District</u>

Ed E. Haynes - engineer (entered service 7-1-71) - No. 1 on seniority list.

Ronnie L. Clark - engineer (entered service 12-18-71)

Billy G. Putnam - #2 on engineer seniority list (8-21-71)

Sam E. Elledge - engineer (8-6-76)

Mike Q. Malone - engineer (7-26-94)
Mike's dad is Milton "Buddy" Malone, retired Southern Railway operator. Mike and wife Melinda have children named Clint, Clay and Emily. They live in Cherokee, Alabama. The editor used to work with Mike's grandad Fred.

W. C. ("Doodle") Murphy - engineer (3-14-73)

Raymond Gene Elliott - engineer (3-14-73)

H. R. Patterson - ("Pat") - engineer (4-27-76)

Danny S. Garner - engineer (2-6-77)

Cary A. Taylor - engineer (2-7-77)

Charlie S. Beckwith - engineer (3-17-77)

Curtis R. Wallace - engineer (8-25-78)

Mark O. Johnson - engineer (11-01-78)

(L) Roy Sizemore - conductor (7-21-72)
(R) Larry D. Thornton - engineer (12-14-78)

Carl F. Young, Jr. - engineer (5-3-79)

Mike K. Quillen - engineer (5-8-79)

George E. Boatwright - engineer (5-28-81)

Mike K. Quillen - engineer (5-8-79)

Al L. Clemons - engineer (5-9-79)

R. Harlon Hallmark - engineer (5-10-79)

W. Gary Utley - ("Big Bird") - engineer (5-11-79)

Steve R. Phillips - engineer (10-17-79)

Arthur C. Winchester - engineer (10-19-79)

Chris D. McAnally - engineer (12-8-80)

A. Dixon Livingston - engineer (2-29-80)

Randy G. Malone - engineer (4-11-80)

Danny T. Hollander - engineer (7-14-80)

195

Tony R. Pace - engineer (7-23-80)

Phillip W. Crowe - engineer (10-21-80)

Mike W. Hill - engineer (7-17-81)

(L) Steve Pickering - ("Pick") - conductor (2-3-79)
(R) G. Kenny Gooch - engineer (10-31-88)

Harry S. Deloach - engineer (6-28-88)

Ricky D. Kelley - engineer (6-28-88)

M. Hugh Brown, II - engineer (10-31-88)

Ronald M. Steen - engineer (10-31-88)

Stephen M. Davidson - engineer (11-01-88)

Bobby Joe Goodwin - engineer (11-01-88)

Darnell Byrd - engineer (12-10-91)

J. Steve Hudson - engineer (12-10-91)

Steve E. Rhodes - engineer (7-16-93)

(L) Joe Willis - conductor (3-11-79)
(R) Larry Dixon - engineer (8-6-93)

(L) Percy Miller, Jr. - conductor (7-22-73)
(R) Ronald C. Mills - engineer (10-29-93)

A. Dale Michael - engineer (10-29-93)

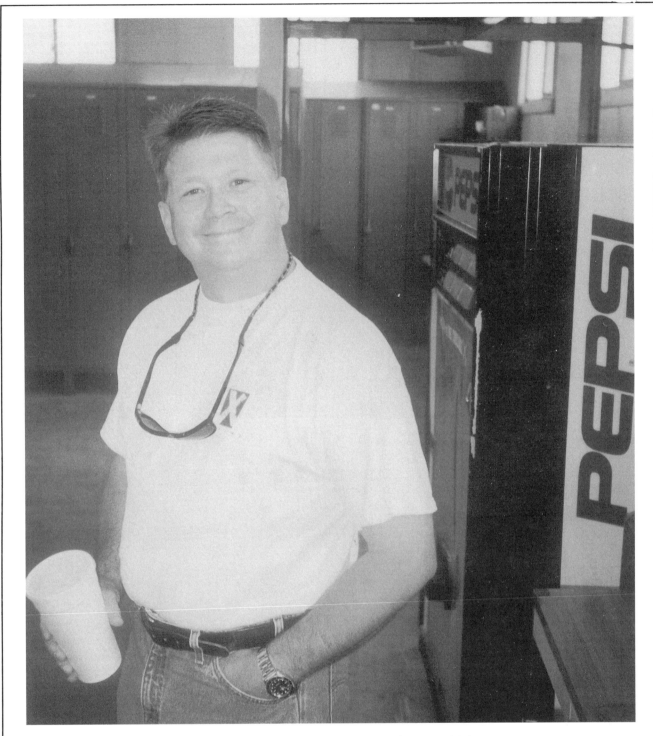

Troy L. Conway, Jr. - engineer (10-29-93)

204

Jeff L. Mayfield - engineer (10-29-93)

J. Randy Curtis - engineer (7-26-94)

(L) Jack H. Landers, Jr. - engineer (11-26-93)
(R) William Earl Martin - conductor (3-12-79)

J. Don Hand - engineer (11-26-93)

Ty R. Thompson - engineer (5-20-94)

George R. Abernathy - engineer (7-26-94)

Terry D. Smith - engineer (7-26-94)

Steve D. Anderson - engineer (7-26-94)

208

Tim O. Mashburn - engineer (7-26-94)

209

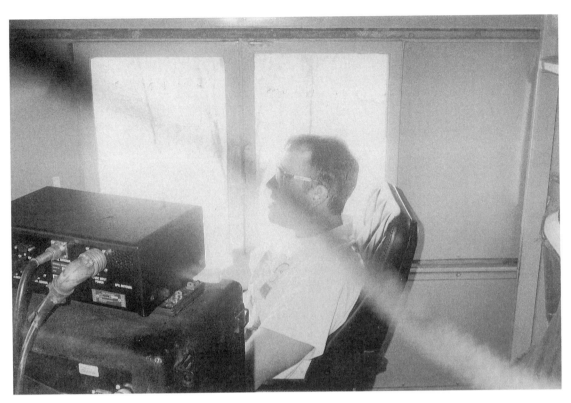

Eric L. Walker - engineeer (7-26-94)

Andy Elledge - engineer (9-22-94)

Tim H. Kent - engineer (12-12-94)

Ronald D. Scott - engineer (3-17-95)

L. Dewayne O'Neill - engineer (3-17-95)

G. Todd Gunnin - engineer (10-30-95)

Phillip D. Murphy - engineer (3-17-95)

(L) Ty R. Thompson - engineer (5-20-94)
(R) Phillip D. Kirk - engineer (4-14-97)

213

J. Paul Creasy - Conductor (8-7-65) No. 1 on seniority list

James E. Bennett - ("Sweeten") - Conductor (10-17-65)

J. C. Kilpatrick - ("Killer") - Conductor (1-9-70)

J. D. Fleming ("Flim-flam") - Conductor (3-31-70)

Luther E. Grisham - Conductor (4-12-70)

M. Mike Jackson ("Skip Jack") - Conductor (5-15-70)

Bobby G. Grisham - Conductor (2-22-71)

Bobby and wife, Shelby, live in Sheffield, AL and have two daughters, Kristi and Tammy.

Our NS Goal-No Damage

Willie E. Pittman - conductor (7-22-73)

Melvyn R. Myhan - conductor (7-22-73)

L. E. Hobson - ("Hobb") Conductor (1-22-73)

G. David McKinney - Brakeman (7-14-72)

G. Steve Pope - ("Quarterback") - Conductor (4-3-76)

Jimmy Larimore - ("Greek") - Conductor (4-8-76)

William A. Softley - conductor (12-7-76)

J. Cliff Wade ("Commadore") - conductor (4-6-78)

**(L) Steve L. Castleberry ("Lefty) - conductor (7-10-78) No longer employed.
(R) J. Tim Baughn - engineer (4-14-97)**

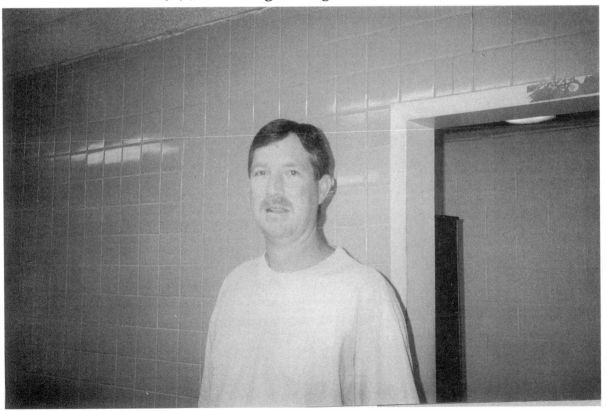

Steve Southern - conductor (7-10-78

Paul D. Pate ("Possum") - conductor (8-4-78)

Larry G. Mansel ("G Man") - conductor (6-12-79)

L. E. Acklin - engineer & conductor (7-10-78)

Mike W. ("Goldfinger") Goodman - conductor (8-4-78)

(L) Charles Douglas Pendley - conductor (11-11-96)
(R) Tom W. Dugger - conductor (7-10-78)

Phillip H. Diremeyer - conductor (10-27-78)

Danny N. Gardner - conductor (12-27-78)

G. Steve Pickering - conductor (2-3-79)

Mike D. Warhurst - conductor (8-3-79)

Phillip D. Wright - engineer (10-20-79)

Ted W. Albright - Conductor (2-3-79)

Willie E. Martin - conductor (3-12-79)

K. Damien Caperton - Conductor (6-15-79)

Tim R. Schell ("Pepper") - conductor (8-27-79)

(L) Wayne A. Berry - conductor (6-28-88)
(R) Barry Moore - conductor (6-28-88)

(L) Robert L. Scott - conductor (6-28-88)
(R) J. J. Jones - conductor (6-28-88)

Ricky Moultrie - conductor (1-18-80)

A. W. Frazier - ("Tony") - conductor (1-18-80)

Jack Oakley, III - conductor (1-18-80)

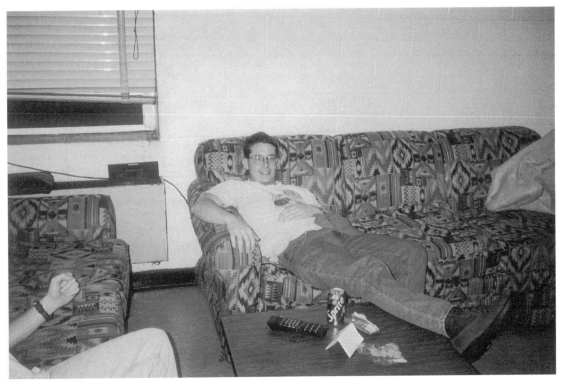

Allen W. McBride - conductor (2-1-94)

Ricky J. Agee - conductor (8-29-79)

Wayne Holt - conductor (9-22-94)

J. Mike Bishop - conductor (6-28-88) Jackson Yard

Glen D. ("Hank") Adderhold - engineer & conductor (11-19-93)

Matt Franks - conductor (2-2-96), now engineer trainee

Kenny Dale Liles - conductor (10-21-96)

Kenneth D. Carter - conductor (11-11-96)

David W. Pendley - conductor (11-11-96)

Jason M. Devaney - conductor (6-28-97)

Thomas S. Clark - conductor (6-28-97)

Phillip Bates - Brakeman (12-31-72)

Ray Dean - Brakeman (1-10-73)

Left: Mike Berry - brakeman (6-28-88)
Right: Randy Mansell - yardmaster, Sheffield (10-27-78)

Todd Sizemore - brakeman (2-2-96),, now engineer trainee. Todd causes the editor to realize that he is getting older as he went to school in Cherokee, AL with Todd's grandmother.

Mike Cook - brakeman (6-27-71)

Railroaders are away from home quite a bit. Most of them keep a car at the opposite terminals for convenience. On July 4, 1997, Matt Franks, NS engineer trainee, Tim Wagnon, NS engineer and Conductor Dave Jordan were out relaxing.

Ricky Moultrie - conductor (1-18-80)

Tim Beard - conductor (3-24-80)

Larry W. Kiser - switchman (6-28-88) Jackson

Neal D. Willingham - brakeman (7-22-73)

Kenneth D. Carter - conductor, now engineer trainee

Jack Landers, Jr. - engineer

P. D. Crowe - engineer.

Ty Thompson - engineer. Came from a long line of railroaders.

244

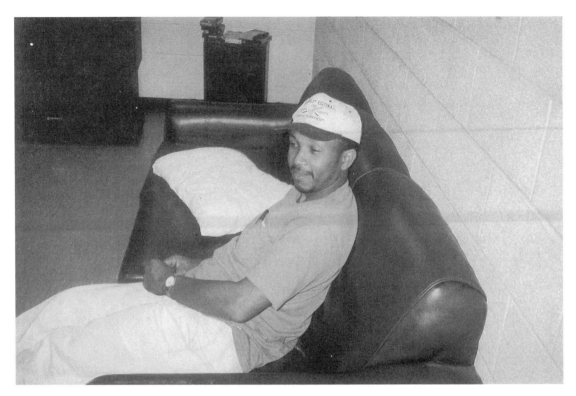

George Abernathy - engineer.

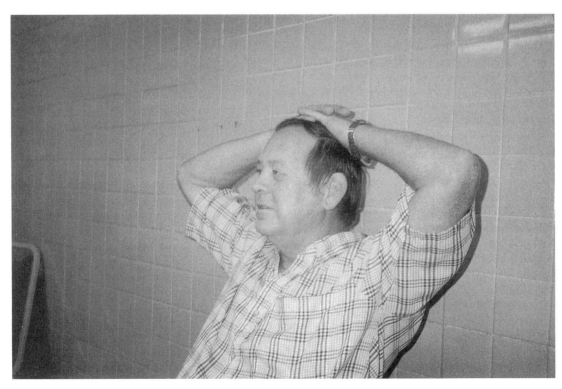

J. D. Fleming - conductor.

Larry McWilliams, the "Fiddling Engineer," has worked for Southern Railway as well as switchman and engineer for Norfolk Southern for twenty-eight years through 1998. He is currently an engineer on the 3:00 p.m. yard engine in Decatur, AL. He is known in many states as the "Fiddling Engineer." Larry has played the fiddle for many well known Bluegrass groups across the country. Among those groups is Jake Landers, writer of the Kentucky Headhunter's hit, "Softly on This Heart of Mine."

Larry McWilliams - engineer (3-17-77)

Raymond Aday, Jr. - engineer (entered service 12-19-76)

John F. Cunningham - conductor (entered service 10-10-73)

Steve D. Anderson - engineer (entered service 7-26-94)

Glendon Farris - engineer (entered servie 5-20-71)

Ted Mitchell - engineer (entered service 3-17-77)

Ronald Scott - engineer (entered service 6-3-91)
Pat Fuller - switchman (entered service 6-11-77)

Steve Flannagan - switchman (entered service 2-5-77)

Ray Dean - brakeman (entered service 1-10-73)

Kent Baggett - yard foreman (entered service 6-13-77)

Dale Copeland - yard foreman (entered service 7-22-73)

Leland W. Kidd - switchman (entered service 8-4-78)

J. Pat Fuller - switchman (entered service 6-11-77)

Kenny Dale Liles - switchman (entered service 5-27-94)

Ed N. Jenkins - switchman (entered service 8-3-79)

Ricky Richardson - yard foreman (entered service 7-22-73)

Milton Cook - conductor (entered service 4-11-78)

Jim Ed Haynes - brakeman (entered service 2-3-79)

Billy Borden - freight agent at Decatur, AL

Greg Lehman - trainmaster, now transferred.

Sonny Wimbs - freight clerk at Decatur, AL

Audrey Bailey - freight clerk at Decatur, AL.

Chris Johnson - freight clerk at Decatur, AL

Steve King - freight clerk at Decatur, AL

Billy Dixon - freight clerk at Decatur, AL

Victor Ashby - freight clerk at Decatur, AL

Jack Baker - track gang foreman at Decatur, AL

Roger Lemay - operator at Decatur, AL

Gary Powell - hump foreman at Decatur, AL

Curtis Putnam, NS yard foreman ar Decatur, AL (entered service 1-10-76)
Gene Clements, NS switchman at Decatur, AL (entered service 4-9-76)
Paul Cook, NS engineer at Decatur, AL (entered service 1-26-78)

W. Dale Smith, NS conductor on east local (entered service 4-17-76)
Larry D. Thornton, NS engineer on east local (entered service 12-14-78)
Ray Dean, NS brakeman on east local (entered service 1-10-73)

Billy Borden - Agent at Decatur, AL

Rick A. Adcock - West end dispatcher in Knoxville, TN

Norfolk Southern Train #202 with engines Rio Grande 6372 and Southern Pacific 7830 at Cherokee, AL on Sept. 8, 1998, with engineer Ed Haynes (No. 1 on engineer's seniority list) and conductor J. C. "Killer" Kilpatrick (No. 3 on conductor's seniority list) nearing the end of their run at 10:45 a.m. Photo by Jack Daniel.

L to R: Conductor Mike Warhurst - engineer Phillip Wright - conductor J. C. Kilpatrick and seated, engineer Willie D. Hutton on September 11, 1998. Mike & Phillip had come into Memphis on train Q35 with lead engine Union Pacific 7120 and J. C. had come in on train 225 with engine NS 9181 and Willie had come in on train 391 with engine NS6203. These fellows were hungry and had Mexican food in mind. Photo by Jack Daniel.

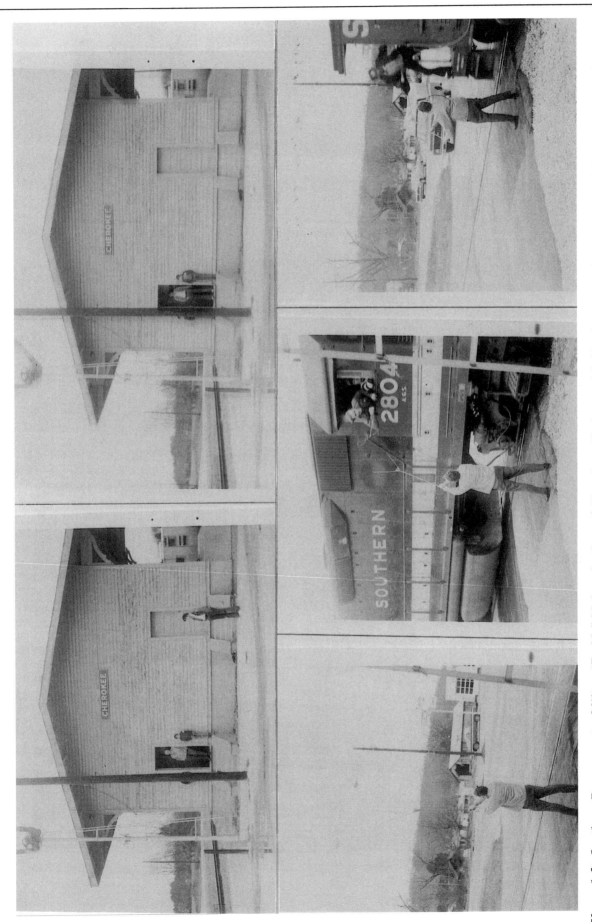

Upper left: Southern Rwy. operator Milton "Buddy" Malone in door of Cherokee, AL depot with his three sons: Steve on ground, Rusty on right of Dad, and Mike on left behind pole. Upper right: Steve in door, Rusty on right and Mike still behind pole. Bottom three photos are of Buddy Malone handing up flemsies to 2nd No. 163 on Feburary 22, 1974. Rusty later became a track man and Mike became a Norfolk Southern engineer. The editor could not find agreement as to who the train crew was. Photo courtesy of Milton and Mike Malone.

Sometimes a good conductor can get more railroading done on the phone than on a locomotive. Pictured here is "Conductor Dave" Jordan doing some railroading.

Two healthy and happy Norfolk Southern railroaders. On left, "Conductor Dave" Jordan and on right, engineer Phillip Crowe

Humping cars by computer. A highly automated classification yard at Sheffield, Alabama. Photo in editor's collection.

The 364 Freight

I run on the NS and carry a grip.
Catch the Dog Law about every trip.
I have a good job, the people say,
For I work by the hour and not by the day.

I left home one trip, the baby could creep;
When I got back, the baby could walk.
I left again, with eight hours sleep,
And when I returned, the baby could talk.

I didn't wish a life of hardship,
But I learned to work both early and late?
When I make trips to Memphis and
bring back NS three-sixty-four freight.

You get your call in the morning
But leave in the evening late.
You were ordered! Ten-thirty for Sheffield
To run the NS three-sixty-four freight.

The weather! Who cares for the weather?
Sometimes it can agitate,
But you'll go just the same or lose your job
Running the three-sixty four freight.

Oh, the heck with it.
Most times the fellowship is great!
When the dispatcher works with me,
The 364 trip I humbly take.

Originally a R. B. Dixon poem but adapted by the editor to fit the NS-Memphis District.

Chapter Five

Today's Railroad Forms

FORM 23-A (Rev. 7/95) (ITEM #113160)

Date _____

NORFOLK SOUTHERN
TRACK TIME FORM 23-A

No. _____ To _____ may use _____track

between _____

and _____

until _____restrictions _____

_____

Time
repeated_____

Time control station
acknowledges report that
specified tracks are clear_____

```
DIST: TN SUB-DIST: SR        TRAINS ENROUTE INQUIRY                    PSTS02N
           POOL:             DESTINATION STATION:
      TRAIN      ON DUTY  ORIGN  <<< LAST OS >>>            CREW INFO
  X   SYMBOL     DATE/TIME STATN STATN/DATE/TIME ETA   ENGINEER   PO CONDUCTOR   PO
      226T601    0402 0005 401A                        LANDERS, J MC PITTMAN, W MC
      Q38T702    0402 0315 547A                        WINCHESTER MC MARTIN, W.  MC
      462T602    0402 0315 401A                        GOODWIN, B MC JORDAN, T.  MC
      481T602    0402 0645 240A                        DAVIDSON,  MC BAUGHN, J.  MC
      T91T802    0402 0800 IC471                       BARNETT, A JL RUSHING, R  JL
      T95T702    0403 0830 459A                        ELLEDGE, S CT SOFTLY, W.  CT
      T74T702    0402 0430 IC471                       SMITH, T.  WL HESTER, D.  WL
      T73T702    0402 0700 401A                        KELLEY, R. WL JONES, J.   WL
      202T702    0402 0525 547A                        WALLACE, C WE OAKLEY, J.  WE
      364T702    0402 0615 547A                        HAND, D. J WE DIRMEYER,   WE
      391T702    0402 0615 401A                        HUTTON, W. WE BENNETT, J  WE
      T81T602    0402 0530 298A                        THORNTON,  SS OAKLEY, B.  SS
      T80T602    0402 0730 401A                        QUILLEN, M SS LARIMORE,   SS
```

This is a **TRAINS ENROUTE INQUIRY** printout from the computer. This information would be of interest to a yardmaster. Any employee with a personal computer has access to this information also. Note the train symbol on left. The 4th & 5th letter designates which part of the Tennessee Division the train is on such as the top train has T6 which, from the table below, indicates it is from Sheffield to Chattanooga.

TENNESSEE DIVISION

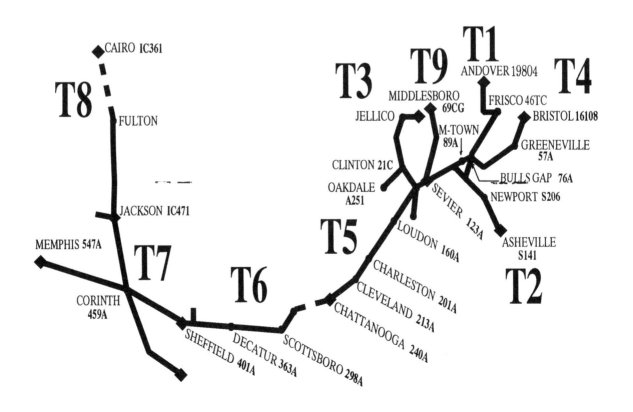

This

Track

Warrant

takes

the

place

of the

old

train

order

forms

19 & 31

FORM 11369 (Rev. 5/95)
(113699)

NORFOLK SOUTHERN
TRACK WARRANT

No. _____   _____ , 19 _____

To: _____ At _____

(Mark "X" in box for each item instructed)

1. ☐Track Warrant No._____of_____is void.

2. ☐Proceed from _____

   To _____

   On _____ Track

3. ☐Work between _____

   and _____

   On _____ Track

4. ☐This authority expires at_____ M.

5. ☐Not in effect until after arrival of _____ _____

   and _____ and _____

   At_____

6. ☐Hold Main Track at last named point.

7. ☐Do not foul limits ahead of _____

   and _____and _____.

8. ☐Clear Main Track at last named point.

9. ☐Between _____&_____
   make all movements at Restricted Speed. Limits occupied
   by train or engine.

10. ☐Between _____&_____
    make all movements at Restricted Speed and stop short
    of men or equipment fouling track.

11. ☐Rule 99 protection not required against following trains on
    same track.

12. ☐Other specific instructions: _____

   _____

   OK _____ M   Dispatcher _____

   Copied By _____

OS Loc _____Date _____ Time_____ By _____

OS Loc _____Date _____ Time_____ By _____

OS Loc _____Date _____ Time_____ By _____

OS Loc _____Date _____ Time_____ By _____

OS Loc _____Date _____ Time_____ By _____

   Limits Reported Clear at _____ **M**

   By _____

NORFOLK SOUTHERN RAILWAY COMPANY

NS NORFOLK SOUTHERN

FORM 2259-1 (Rev. 3/96)
(Item 160674)

BLOCK CONSIST

TRAIN NUMBER	FWD YARD TRACK NO.	YARD	DATE
462T6	74	Sheffal	1-30-97

TIME CALLED	DESTINATION
1015 am	Chatt Term

ENGINES	CABOOSE
8622 6680	

2	3	4	5	6	7	8	10	11
HEAD CAR		REAR CAR			HEAD END			
					BLOCK DESTINATION	LOADS	EMPTY	TONS
INITIAL	NUMBER	INITIAL	NUMBER					
				X				
SRN	1292	Cext	620085	X	Chatt P	65	16	7555
				X				
				X				
				X				
				X				
				X				
				X				
				X				
				X				

LOADED TANKS	☑ YES ☐ NO	OPEN-TOP HOPPERS	☐ YES ☐ NO	☐ L ☐ E	TRAIN TOTAL	65	16	7555

HIGH & WIDE	☐ YES ☑ NO	PROPERLY CLEARED	☐ YES ☐ NO — Explain:

HAZARDOUS MATERIALS	☑ YES ☐ NO	IF YES SEE FORM 2259HM, FORM 870 or FORM 870PG.

31, 34, 61, from Engr

PERISHABLES	☐ YES ☑ NO	EMPTY B. HEAD FLATS	☐ YES ☑ NO
		EMPTY WOOD RACKS	☐ YES ☑ NO
		AIR DUMP CARS	☐ YES ☑ NO
		OTHER (DESCRIBE)	☐ YES ☑ NO

CONNECTING WAYBILLS OBSERVED	☐ YES ☑ NO	

REMARKS	CLERK
	W

NORFOLK SOUTHERN   END—OF—TRIP FORM   FORM 11498 (REV. 1/97) (Item 114986)

TRAIN:_____ OF ___/___/___ - _____ P   DEPARTURE: _____

ARRIVED YARD BOARD -   DATE: ___/___/___   TIME: _____   STATION TRAIN LEFT AT: _____

ENTERED FINAL TRACK: _____ STOPPED FINAL TRACK: _____ RELIEVED TRACK: _____

ORIGIN STATION: _____ INTERMEDIATE STATIONS: _____ _____ FINAL STATION: _____

RADIOS: _____ _____   RETURN TRAIN IDS: _____ _____ _____

LOADS: _____ EMPTIES: _____ TONS: _____ CARS HANDLED: _____ MAX CARS: _____

ENGINES: _____

: _____

TIME ENGINEER BOARDED ENGINE _____

EMPLOYEE NAME	CC	On Duty	REL RESP Date	Time	OFF DUTY Date	Time	10 Hr	Miles	WkBeg	CO SV	Phone

TRAIN DELAYS

	Milepost	HHMM	Code	Units	ADDITIONAL REMARKS
1					
2					
3					
4					
5					
6					
7					
8					
9					
10					
11					
12					

DELAY CODES

ACP - Accident-Protected Crossing
1 CRC - Radio Control Unit Failure
MBE - Brakes in Emergency
MIB - Inspection and Brake Test
1 MSO - S/O B/O Car in Yard
1 MUN - Train Uncoupled
STA - Detector Stop-No Cause Found
* TAH - Train Ahead
TCE - Crew Eat
TDB - Double & Couple Train
TDN - Drug Screen - NS
TET - End of Train Device
THL - Train Helping Train
TIC - Rd Crew Handle Interchange
* TMT - Meet Train
TPR - Pick up and Make Radio
TRT - Reduce Train
TSO - Set off
TST - Train Stalled
TWG - Weighing Train

ACU - Accident-Unprotected Crossing
ESO - Slow Orders
1 MDE - Dragging Equipment
1 MMF - Engine Failure
1 MSR - S/O B/O Car on Road
SPS - Power Switch Failure
SXM - Crossing Protection Malfunction
TBI - Build Train Init Terminal
TCL - Rd Crew Classifying Cars
TDE - Detour
TDT - Deradio Train
TFE - Fuel & Service Engines
THO - Held Out
TIN - Rd Crew Switch Intermodal
TPF - Pusher Off
TPU - Pick Up
TSE - Swap Engines
TSP - Set off & Pick Up
TTX - Wait on Taxi
TYT - Yarding Train

ADE - Derailment
MBA - Burst Air Hose
1 MHB - Hot Box
1 MSA - Air Hose Separation
1 MTL - Train Line
SST - Signal Trouble
* TAD - Train Ahead Derailed
1 TBR - Hand Brake
TCS - Swap Crews
TDF - Drug Screen - FRA
TDW - Train Delay Weather
THE - Wait on Helper Engine
THT - Heavy Train on Grade
TML - Rd Crew Switch Multilevels
TPO - Pusher On
TRC - Rule Check
TSI - Rd Crew Switch Industry
TSR - Swap Radio Units
TTY - Pull Thru Yard

NOTES: 1 - Need Car Initial and Number in the ADDITIONAL REMARKS FIELD.
* - Need Symbol of Train in the ADDITIONAL REMARKS FIELD.

Norfolk Southern

LOCOMOTIVE SERIES TABLE

Road Nos	Model	Road Nos	Model
50-59	SD9M	4100-4159	GP38AC
67-83	SW1500	4600-4605	GP49
100-104	TC10	4606-4641	GP59
115-116	F40PH	5000-5256	GP38-2
1002-1012	SW1	6073-6206	SD40-2
1209	SW12	6500-6505	SD50
1357-1388	GP40	6506-6525	SD50
1580-1624	SD40	6550-6700	SD60
1625-1652	SD40-2	7000-7002	GP40X
1733	SW1500	7003-7092	GP50
2105	SW1	7101-7150	GP60
2290-2347	SW1500	8003-8082	C30-7
2348-2435	MP15	8500-8542	C36-7
2501-2556	SD70	8550-8563	C39-8
2717-2822	GP38	8564-8688	C39-8
2823-2878	GP38AC	8689-8763	D8-40C
2879-2886	GP38	8764-8888	D9-40C
3170-3200	SD40	9710-9713	RP-E4
3201-3328	SD40-2	9714-9741	RP-E4D
3500-3521	B30-7A	9819-9820	RP-F4U
3522-3566	D8-32B	9834	RP-E4U
3815-3820	B36-7	9835-9841	RP-A4U
3900-3969	U23B	9842-9855	RP-E4U
3970-4023	B23-7	9902-9919	RP-F6Y
		9920-9923	RP-E6Y

STAND-ALONE DETECTORS

Memphis East End District	Memphis West End District	Jackson District
Wauhatchie	Scott	Martin
Fackler	Cherokee	Sharon
Scottsboro	Oldham	Bradford
Limrock	Burnsville	Sitka
Paint Rock	Oakland	Oakfield
Ryland	Wenasoga	Perry
Huntsville	Pocahontas	Henderson
Greenbrier	Candlewood	McNairy
Irvington	LaGrange	Falcon
Hillsboro	Hays	Guys
Courtland	Collierville	
Town Creek	Germantown	

Norfolk Southern

DIESEL UNIT RATING IN TONS

	C36-7 C39-8 D8-40C D9-40C SD50 SD60 SD70	C30-7 SD40	B30-7A B36-7 D8-32B GP40X GP49 GP50 GP59 GP60	B23-7 GP38 GP40 U23B

WESTWARD

Memphis East End District

deButts - Stevenson	4500	3250	2750	2050
Stevenson - Huntsville	6350	4650	3850	2900
Huntsville - Decatur	7050	5110	4250	3200
Decatur - Sheffield	10200	7450	6200	4650

Memphis West End District

Sheffield - Margerum	6700	4850	4050	3050
Margerum - Corinth	5150	3750	3150	2350
Corinth - Grand Jct.	6800	4950	4150	3100
Grand Jct. - Forest yard	11200	8150	6800	5100

Jackson District

Corinth - Jackson	7700	5600	4650	3500
Jackson - Fulton	5250	3850	3200	2400
Bemis - Iselin Jct.	3750	2700	2300	1700
Bemis - Poplar Corner	3750	2700	2300	1700

EASTWARD

Memphis East End District

Sheffield - Decatur	8800	6400	5350	4000
Decatur - Huntsville	6500	4700	3950	2950
Huntsville - Chase	4950	3600	3000	2250
Chase - Stevenson	10650	7750	6450	4850
Stevenson - deButts	4300	3100	2600	1950

Memphis West End District

Forest yard - Grand Jct.	5700	4150	3450	2600
Grand Jct.- Corinth	7450	5450	4550	3400
Corinth - Margerum	5700	4150	3450	2600
Margerum - Sheffield	7700	5600	4650	3500

MEMPHIS DISTRICT EAST END—WESTWARD

Capacity of Tracks		MILE POST	STATIONS	SEE PAGE 1	INTERLOCKINGS	RR CROSSING SEE SPEC. INST.	SECTION 3	MILES FROM BRISTOL
Other Tracks In Cars	Sidings In Feet							
Yard	..	240.0A	Y..deButts Yd..DN		..		◇	240.0
....	....	241.8A	......Pratt......	‖	C			241.8
....	....	242.6A	...C. T. Tower...	‖	C			242.6
....	....	245.2A	..North Tunnel..	‖				245.2
....	....	246.1A	..South Tunnel..					246.1
....	....	248.1A	...Wauhatchie...	*	C			248.1
Yard	....	280.0A	YL Y.Stevenson..	*	C			280.0
....	7830	281.1A	.Stevenson Sdg..	†				281.1
40	3179	297.6A	...Scottsboro...	†				297.6
....	8198	304.2A	....Midway....	†				304.2
23	....	318.1A	...Paint Rock...	†				318.1
9	....	322.3A	.....Gurley.....	†				322.3
....	4665	324.5A	......Asa......	†				324.5
Yard	....	338.9A	....Huntsville....	†				338.9
....	3894	339.5A	..Huntsville Sdg..	†				339.5
50	10188	343.1A	......Elko......	†				343.1
....	....	348.5A	....Madison....	†				348.5
....	....	362.1A	...Decatur Jct...	†	C			362.1
Yard	....	363.3A	...Decatur...DN		C			363.3
....	9607	364.2A	...Decatur Sdg...	†				364.2
....	7804	379.4A	....Wheeler....	†				379.4
....	....	382.9A	....Courtland....	†				382.9
12	....	388.6A	...Town Creek...	†				388.6
15	....	395.9A	....Leighton....	†				395.9
Yard	....	401.0A	YL Y.Sheffield Yd.DN	†	..			401.0

Alabama Division Timetable governs between deButts (M.P. 240.0A) and Wauhatchie (M.P. 248.1A). *CSXT Timetable and Rules govern between Wauhatchie (M.P. 248.1A) and Stevenson (M.P. 279.8A).

MEMPHIS DISTRICT WEST END—WESTWARD

Capacity of Tracks		MILE POST	STATIONS	SEE PAGE 1	INTERLOCKINGS	RR CROSSING SEE SPEC. INST.	SECTION 3	MILES FROM BRISTOL
Other Tracks In Cars	Sidings In Feet							
Yard	....	401.0A	YL Y.Sheffield Yd.DN		..			401.0
....	....	402.8A	Y {..Wilson.....	†	C			402.8
....	....		{..Norala......		C			
....	....		.E. End Two Trks..	†				
....	....		...Tuscumbia...	††				
....	....	412.8A	......Scott......		C			412.8
....	....	413.8A	......Carlin......					413.8
60	6755	415.2A	......Pride......	†				415.2
85	3494	422.7A	Y ...Cherokee...	†				422.7
36	....	428.1A	....Margerum....	†				428.1
....	8932	430.1A	...Oldham.....	†				430.1
9	4788	436.5A	Y......Iuka.....	†				436.5
85	....	444.1A	...Burnsville....	†				444.1
4	10217	448.8A	......Glens......	†				448.8
....	....	457.3A	...Rudy......		C			457.3
85	....	458.8A	Y....Corinth....	† †	A		◇	458.8
4	8962	466.3A	....Chewalla....	†				466.3
10	8937	480.6A	....Middleton....	†				480.6
15	....	494.2A	....Saulsbury....	†				494.2
60	....	499.9A	Y .Grand Junction.	†				499.9
....	10301	505.4A	.....Rather.....	†				505.4
12	8995	521.1A	....Rossville....	†				521.1
37	1699	527.9A	....Collierville....	†				527.9
6	....	537.2A	...Germantown...	†				537.2
....	7609	540.1A	...White Siding...	†				540.1
....	....	546.3A	..Buntyn.....		C			546.3
Yard	....	547.0A	YL {.Forrest Yd DN	§§				547.0
....	....	549.9A	. K. C. Junction	§§			◇	549.9
Yard	....	552.3A	...Memphis..	§§				552.3

Rossville siding should be 8687 feet instead of 8995 as shown.

Appendix
Norfolk Southern
Seniority Lists

Norfolk Southern engineer, J. Randy Curtis, entered service 7-26-94. Photo by Barry Boothe.

NORFOLK SOUTHERN RAILROAD
TENNESSEE DIVISION (MEMPHIS / CHATTANOOGA SECTION)
CONDUCTORS BY DATE OF PROMOTION

	Name	Nickname	Assignmt	Conduct	Brakem	
01.	J. Paul Creasy		we06	12-17-69	08-07-65	
02.	James E. Bennett	Sweeten	we01	12-17-69	10-17-65	
03.	J. C. Kilpatrick	Killer	we08	10-28-71	01-09-70	
04.	J. D. Fleming	Flim-flam	we03	10-28-71	03-31-70	
05.	Luther E. Grisham		we09	10-28-71	04-12-70	
06.	R. Mike Jackson	Skip Jack	we04	10-28-71	05-15-70	
07.	Bobby G. Grisham		we10	11-11-73	02-22-71	
08.	T. David Jordan	Cond.Dave	mc05	04-09-76	07-16-72	
09.	G. Steve Pope	Quarterback	el42 (Emco)	06-26-77	04-03-76	
10.	Jimmy Larimore	Greek	ss01 (Scottsb)	06-26-77	04-08-76	
11.	W. Dale Smith		ss02 (Scottsb)	06-26-77	04-17-76	
12.	Don A. Hester		wl01 (west)	01-30-78	05-22-76	
13.	W. A. Softley		ct95 (Collv'lle)	04-17-79	12-07-76	
14.	J. Cliff Wade	Commando	we05	06-12-79	04-06-78	
15.	Steve L. Castleberry	Lefty	mc08	06-12-79	07-10-78	off
16.	B. D. Grisham (trainmaster)			06-12-79	07-10-78	
17.	Tom W. Dugger		ee01	06-12-79	07-10-78	
18.	L. L. Richardson (injury)			10-18-79	08-04-78	
19.	C.Steve Southern		we07	03-24-80	07-10-78	
20.	R. K. Mansell	Red	we02	03-24-80	10-27-78	
21.	Danny N. Gardner	Big Dummy	mc01	03-24-80	12-27-78	
22.	G. Steve Pickering	Pick	mc02	03-24-80	02-03-79	
23.	Tim W. Beard		mc06	03-24-80	02-03-79	
24.	K. Damien Caperton	Domino	ee05	08-06-81	06-15-79	
25.	Mike D. Warhurst	Mad Dog	mc03	08-06-81	08-03-79	
26.	E. B. Dixon (medical)			08-06-81	08-29-79	
27.	Greg F. Crowe		mc07	12-28-87	07-10-78	
28.	Ted W. Albright	Teddy	mc10	12-28-87	02-03-79	
29.	Willie E. Martin		mc09	12-28-87	03-12-79	
30.	Larry G. Mansel	G-man	mc11	12-28-87	06-12-79	
31.	Tim R. Schell	Pepper	ee06	12-28-87	08-27-79	
32.	E. Molly Stansell, Sr.		jl92	06-28-88	06-28-88	
33.	R. H. Rushing		jl91	06-28-88	06-28-88	
34.	J. J. Jones		wl02	06-28-88	06-28-88	
35.	J. Mike. Bishop		jl90	06-28-88	06-28-88	
36.	Jimmy N. Collins		ex02c2	06-28-88	06-28-88	
37	Don R. Stegall		ex01c2	06-28-88	06-28-88	
38.	Wayne A. Berry		mc04	06-28-88	06-28-88	
39.	Robert L. Scott		mc12	06-28-88	06-28-88	
40.	J. M. Willis		mc13	07-01-90	03-11-79	
41.	R. J. Agee		x-bd26	07-01-90	08-29-79	
42.	R. R. Moultrie	Ricardo	mc14	07-01-90	01-18-80	
43.	Milton Cook, Jr.		dl89	06-06-91	04-11-78	
44.	L. E. Hobson	Hobb	ee02	01-02-92	01-22-73	
45.	W. E. Pittman	Willie	x-bd12	01-02-92	07-22-73	
46.	Percy B. Miller, Jr.		x-bd16	01-02-92	07-22-73	
47.	Melvyn R. Myhan		x-bd04	01-02-92	07-22-73	
48.	Paul D. Pate	Possum	x-bd06	01-02-92	08-04-78	
49.	Mike W. Goodman	Goldfinger	ee04	01-02-92	08-04-78	
50.	Phillip H. Diremeyer		x-bd11	01-02-92	10-27-78	
51.	A. W. Frazier	Tony	ee03	01-02-92	01-08-80	

NORFOLK SOUTHERN RAILROAD
Tennessee Division (Chattanooga / Memphis Section)
CONDUCTORS BY DATE OF PROMOTION

	Name	Nickname	Assignmt	Cond. date	Brake. date
52.	Jack Oakley, III		x-bd03	01-02-92	01-18-80
53	J. Randy Curtis		x-bd15	01-02-92	
54	Tim H. Kent		x-bd19	01-02-92	
55.	Ronald D. Scott		x-bd24	01-02-92	06-03-91
56.	L. Dewayne Oneill	Big O	x-bd07	01-02-92	06-03-91
57.	Phillip D. Murphy		x-bd27	01-02-92	06-03-91
58.	B. L. Oakley		x-bd01	01-02-92	06-03-91
59.	G. Todd Gunnin		x-bd05	11-19-93	11-19-93
60.	G. D. Adderhold	Hank	x-bd28	11-19-93	11-19-93
61	Allen W. McBride		x-bd08	02-01-94	
62.	P. D. Kirk	Minor	x-bdsh01	09-22-94	09-22-94
63.	J. Tim Baughn		x-bd17	09-22-94	09-22-94
64.	Matt Franks		trainee	02-02-96	
65.	Robert Hawkins		trainee	11-11-96	

Information in a different format provided by Mike D. Warhurst

NORFOLK SOUTHERN RAILROAD
Memphis, Jackson (IC) & N. A. Sub-districts
SENIORITY LIST
ENGINEERS

	NAME	DATE	ASSIGNMENT
1.	Ed E. Haynes	07-01-71	we08
2.	Billy G. Putnam	08-21-71	el42
3.	Ronnie L. Clark	12-18-71	we01
4.	Paul M. Hinton	09-16-72	ytss41
5.	Willie D. Hutton	03-14-73	we11
6.	W. C. Murphy	03-14-73	we06
7.	Raymond G. Elliott	03-14-73	we03
8.	H. R. "Pat" Patterson	04-27-76	we09
10.	Sam E. Elledge	08-06-76	ctct95
12.	Brad E. Riley	02-01-77	ytss01
13.	G. Al Porter	02-01-77	ytfs01
14.	John D. Blaylock	02-01-77	ytss02
15.	Jerry W. Olivis	02-01-77	ytss20
16.	John C. Zabrisky	02-01-77	ytss05
17.	Glendon H. Farris	02-01-77	ytds01
18.	Johnny E. Walker	02-01-77	xtss61
19.	Alfred Mays, Jr.	02-01-77	xtfs60
20.	Danny S. Garner	02-06-77	eeee05
21.	Cary A. Taylor	02-07-77	we04
22.	Charlie S. Beckwith	03-17-77	we05
23.	Ted E. Mitchell	03-17-77	ytss21
24.	Larry W. McWilliams	03-17-77	ytds20
25.	Curtis R. Wallace	08-25-78	we12
26.	Mark O. Johnson	11-01-78	wlwl01
27.	Larry D. Thornton	12-14-78	ssss02
28.	C. F. Young, Jr.	05-03-79	we02
29.	Ronnie N. Ross	05-07-79	ytss40
30.	Mike K. Quillen	05-08-79	ssss01
31.	Al L. Clemons	05-09-79	we10
32.	R. Harlon Hallmark	05-10-79	ee04
33.	W. Gary Utley	05-11-79	mcmc02
34.	Lance K. Underwood	06-18-79	xtds60
35.	Raymond Aday, Jr.	07-20-79	dldl89
36.	Steve R. Phillips	10-17-79	mcmc01
37.	Mike E. Myhan	10-18-79	xtss62
38.	Arthur C. Winchester	10-19-79	mcmc09
39.	Phillip D. Wright	10-20-79	mcmc03
40.	Paul E. Cook	02-19-80	ytds40
41.	Steve E. Collingsworth	02-26-80	ex01
42.	A. Dixon Livingston	02-29-80	ee01
43.	Randy G. Malone	04-11-80	we07
44..	Tony R. Pace	07-23-80	mcmc14
45.	Gary L. Davis	10-20-80	(off)
46.	Phillip W. Crowe	10-21-80	mcmc05
47.	Chris D. McAnally	12-02-80	ee06
48.	George E. Boatwright	05-28-81	ee03

NORFOLK SOUTHERN RAILROAD
Memphis, Jackson (IC) & N. A. Sub-districts
SENIORITY LIST
ENGINEERS

	NAME	DATE	ASSIGNMENT
49.	Nick B. Smithers	07-14-81	ytfs40
50.	D. E. Cheathan	07-14-81	official
51.	Danny T. Hollander	07-14-81	mcmc10
52.	Mike W. Hill	07-17-81	mcmc08
53.	Tim R. Wagnon	07-17-81	mcmc06
54.	B. N. Alexander	06-28-88	jljl91
56.	Jimmy L. Sims	06-28-88	jljl90
57.	Wayne W. Rogers	06-28-88	jljl92
58.	Harry S. Deloach	06-28-88	ex01e2
59.	A. Buck Barnett	06-28-88	ex02e2
60.	Ricky D. Kelley	06-28-88	wlwl02
61.	M. Hugh Brown, II	10-31-88	ex12e1
62.	G. Kenny Gooch	10-31-88	mcmc13
63.	Ronald M. Steen	10-31-88	ex02e1
64.	Jimmy M. Askew	11-01-88	nana02
65.	Danny D. Barker	11-01-88	plpl01
66.	J. G. Hamm	11-01-88	disabled
67.	Wendel K. Olive	11-01-88	nana01
68.	Leo Johnson	11-01-88	nana03
69.	H. C. Hawkins	11-01-88	(promoted)
70.	J. J. Carter	11-01-88	(disabled)
72.	W. E. Wallace	11-01-88	(promoted)
73.	Danny L. Pickett	11-01-88	nana08
74.	L. M. "Doc" Stafford	11-01-88	ex17e6
75.	J. D. Waid	11-01-88	(promoted)
76.	Dave A. Thornton	11-01-88	shsh01
77.	L. M. "Pete" Futrell	11-01-88	nana06
78.	Greg N. Flanagan	11-01-88	nana04
79.	Stephen M. Davidson	11-01-88	mcmc11
80.	Mike E. Worsham	11-01-88	ex05e6
81.	Johnny L. Badgett	11-01-88	ex01e6
82.	J. R. Balentine	11-01-88	ex32e6
83.	Bobby Joe Goodwin	11-01-88	ex12e6
84.	Darnell Byrd	12-10-91	mcmc04
85.	J. Steve Hudson	12-10-91	mcmc07
86.	Alan K. Colglazier	01-04-92	ex02e6
88.	Paul L. Hubbert	03-25-93	ex30e6
89.	Steve E. Rhodes	07-16-93	mcmc12
90.	Larry D. Dixon	08-06-93	ex07e1
91.	Danny L. Weeks	10-29-93	ex31e6
92.	Ronald C. Mills	10-29-93	ex05e1
93.	Jeff L. Mayfield	10-29-93	ex08e1
94.	A. Dale Michael	10-29-93	ex31e1
95.	Troy L. Conway, Jr.	10-29-93	ex09e1
96.	Jack H. Landers, Jr.	11-26-93	ex30e1
97.	J. Don Hand	11-26-93	ex06e1
98.	C. Alan Rickard	11-26-93	ex13e6

NORFOLK SOUTHERN RAILROAD
Memphis, Jackson (IC) & N. A. Sub-districts
SENIORITY LISTS
ENGINEERS

	NAME	DATE	ASSIGNMENT
99.	Greg A. Hill	04-10-94	ex22e6
100.	Ty R. Thompson	05-20-94	ex10e1
101.	Eric L. Walker	07-26-94	ex15e1
102.	George R. Abernathy	07-26-94	ex11e1
103.	Terry D. Smith	07-26-94	ex13e1
104.	Steve D. Anderson	07-26-94	ex03e1
105.	Tim O. Mashburn	07-26-94	ex04e1
106.	Mike Q. Malone	07-26-94	ex01e1
107.	J. Randy Curtis	07-26-94	ex19e1
108.	Tim H. Kent	12-12-94	ex18e1
109.	Ronald D. Scott	03-17-95	ex24c1 (conductor)
110.	L. Dewayne Oneill	03-17-95	ex07c1 "
111.	Phillip D. Murphy	03-17-95	ex27c1 "
112.	B. L. Oakley	03-17-95	ex01c1 "
113.	G. Todd Gunnin	10-30-95	ex05c1 "
114.	Tommy E. Beard	10-31-95	ex03c6 "
115.	G. D. Adderhold	10-31-95	ex28c1 "
116.	C. Matt Sellers	05-24-96	xtfs60s1 (switchman)
117.	Allen W. McBride	10-21-96	ex08c1 (conductor)
118.	Edward H. Wilson	10-21-96	ytfs20
119.	Kenny D. Liles	10-21-96	ex09sw (switchman)
121.	Phillip D. Kirk	04-14-97	ex02c1 (conductor)
122.	J. Tim Baughn	04-14-97	ex17c1 (conductor)

(Information in a different format provided by Tim W. Wagnon - NS Engineer on July 7, 1997)

ROSTER DESCRIPTION: MEMPHIS DIST ROAD CONDR

X	RANK	DATE	EMPLOYEE NAME		ASGNMENT	STATUS
	10	691217	CREASY, J. P.	(PAUL)	WEWE06CO	OFF
	20	691217	BENNETT, J. E.	(JAMES)	WEWE01CO	
	40	711028	KILPATRICK, J. C.	(PAT)	WEWE08CO	
	50	711028	FLEMING, J. D.	(JD)	WEWE03CO	
	60	711028	GRISHAM, L. E.	(LUTHER)	WEWE09CO	OFF
	70	711028	JACKSON, R. M.	(MIKE)	WEWE04CO	
	80	731111	GRISHAM, B. G.	(BOBBY)	MCMC05CO	
	110	760409	JORDAN, T. D.	(DAVID)	MCMC05CO	
	120	760409	YOUNG, C. F. JR.	(SMOOTH)	WEWE10EN	OFF
	130	770205	UTLEY, W. G.	(GARY)	WEWE02EN	
	140	770205	CLEMONS, A. L.	(AL)	WEWE07EN	
	150	770626	POPE, G. S.	(STEVE)	ELEL42CO	
	160	770626	LARIMORE, J.	(JIMMY)	SSSS01CO	
	170	770626	UNDERWOOD, L. K.	(LANCE)	XTDS60EN	
	180	770626	SMITH, W. D.	(DALE)	SSSS02CO	OFF
	190	780130	HESTER, D. A.	(DON)	WLWL01CO	
	200	780130	MYHAN, M. E.	(MIKE)	XTSS62EN	
	210	790417	SOFTLY, W. A.	(WILLIAM)	CTCT95CO	

ENTER=INQ/RSTRT   PF3=EXIT   PF4=SENIORITY MOVE   PF7=UP   PF8=DN
PRESS PFKEY8 TO SEE MORE

SENIORITY ROSTER INQUIRY

ROSTER CODE: AB   EMP-NBR: DIST: SDIST:

ROSTER DESCRIPTION: MEMPHIS DIST ROAD CONDR

X	RANK	DATE	EMPLOYEE NAME		ASGNMENT	STATUS
	220	790612	WADE, J. C.	(CLIFF)	WEWE05CO	OFF
	240	790612	GRISHAM, B. D.			
	250	790612	DUGGER, T. W.	(TOM)	EEEE01CO	
	260	791018	RICHARDSON, L. L.	(LANDEL)		OFF
	270	800324	SOUTHERN, C. S.	(STEVE)	WEWE07CO	
	280	800324	MANSELL, R. K.	(RANDY)	WEWE02CO	
	290	800324	GARDNER, D. N.	(DANNY)	MCMC01CO	
	300	800324	PICKERING, G. S.	(STEVE)	MCMC02CO	
	310	800324	SMITHERS, N. B.	(NICK)	YTFS40EN	
	320	800324	BEARD, T. W.	(TIM)	MCMC06CO	
	330	810806	HAND, D. J.	(DON)	EX0006E1	
	340	810806	CAPERTON, K. D.	(DAMIEN)	EEEE05CO	
	350	810806	REAVES, J. L.	(JAMES)		OFF
	360	810806	WARHURST, M. D.	(MIKE)	MCMC03CO	
	370	810806	DIXON, E. B.	(ED)	DISMISS	OFF
	390	871228	BYRD, D.	(DARNELL)	MCMC04EN	
	400	871228	ACKLIN, L. E. SR.	(LEWIS)	MCMC15CO	
	410	871228	CROWE, G. F.	(GREG)	MCMC07CO	

ENTER=INQ/RSTRT   PF3=EXIT   PF4=SENIORITY MOVE   PF7=UP   PF8=DN

ROSTER DESCRIPTION: MEMPHIS DIST ROAD CONDR

X	RANK	DATE	EMPLOYEE NAME		ASGNMENT	STATUS
	420	871228	ALBRIGHT, T. W.	(TED)	MCMC10CO	
	430	871228	MARTIN, W. E.	(WILLIE)	MCMC09CO	
	440	871228	MANSELL, L. G.	(LARRY)	MCMC11CO	
	450	871228	LANDERS, J. H. JR	(JACK)	EX0030E1	
	460	871228	HUDSON, J. S.	(STEVE)	MCMC07EN	
	470	871228	SCHELL, T. R.	(TIM)	EEEE06CO	
	480	880628	STANSELL, E. M. SR	(MOLLY)	JLJL92CO	

```
490 880628 RUSHING, R. H.          (RH)    JLJL91C0
500 880628 ARNETT, C. D.      (CHARLES)    JLJL92B1
510 880628 COLLINS, J. N.       (JIMMY)    EX0002C2
520 880628 STEGALL, D. R.        (DON)     EX0001C2
530 880628 BEARD, B. S. JR.    (BENNY)     JLJL91B1
540 880628 JONES, J. J.           (JJ)     WLWL02C0     VACATI(
550 880628 BISHOP, J. M.        (MIKE)     JLJL90C0
570 880628 HOLLEY, C. T.                   DISABLED     OFF
580 880628 BERRY, W. A.        (WAYNE)     MCMC04C0
590 880628 KISER, L. W.           (LW)     JLJL90B1
600 880628 SCOTT, R. L.       (ROBERT)     MCMC12C0
ENTER=INQ/RSTRT  PF3=EXIT  PF4=SENIORITY MOVE  PF7=UP    PF8=DN
PRESS PFKEY8 TO SEE MORE
                     SENIORITY ROSTER INQUIRY
    ROSTER CODE: AB   EMP-NBR:        DIST:       SDIST:
         ROSTER DESCRIPTION: MEMPHIS DIST ROAD CONDR
X  RANK    DATE        EMPLOYEE NAME          ASGNMENT    STATUS
  610 880628 MOORE, B. E.        (BARRY)     EX0012B1
  620 890524 COWART, T. U.        (TUCK)     DISABLED     OFF
  630 890524 BERRY, J. M.         (MIKE)     WLWL02B1
  640 900701 MICHAEL, A. D.       (DALE)     EX0031E1
  650 900701 HAYNES, E. E.          (ED)     WEWE08EN
  660 900701 PORTER, G. A.          (AL)     YTFS01EN
  670 900701 PUTNAM, B. G.       (BILLY)     ELEL42EN     VACATI(
  680 900701 CLARK, R. L.       (RONNIE)     WEWE01EN
  690 900701 WILLIS, J. M.         (JOE)     MCMC13C0
  700 900701 HINTON, P. M.        (PAUL)     YTSS41EN
  710 900701 AGEE, R. J.          (RICK)     MCMC08C0     VACATIO
  720 900701 HUTTON, W. D.      (WILLIE)     WEWE11EN
  730 900701 MOULTRIE, R. R.     (RICKY)     MCMC14C0
  740 900701 MURPHY, W. C.          (WC)     WEWE06EN
  750 900701 MILLS, R. C.       (RONALD)     MCMC08EN
  760 900701 ELLIOTT, R. G.    (RAYMOND)     WEWE03EN
  770 900701 THOMPSON, T. R.        (TY)     EX0010E1
  780 900701 PATTERSON, H. R.      (PAT)     WEWE09EN
ENTER=INQ/RSTRT  PF3=EXIT  PF4=SENIORITY MOVE   PF7=UP   PF8=DN
X  RANK    DATE        EMPLOYEE NAME          ASGNMENT    STATUS
  800 900701 ELLEDGE, S. E.       (SAM)      CTCT95EN
  820 900701 RILEY, B. E.        (BRAD)      YTSS01EN
  830 900701 BLAYLOCK, J. D.     (JOHN)      YTSS02EN
  840 900701 OLIVIS, J. W.      (JERRY)      YTSS05EN     OFF
  850 900701 ZABRISKY, J. C.     (JOHN)      YTSS20EN
  860 900701 FARRIS, G. H.    (GLENDON)      YTDS01EN
  870 900701 WALKER, J. E.     (JOHNNY)      XTSS61EN
  880 900701 MAYES, A. JR.     (ALFRED)      XTFS60EN     OFF
  890 900701 GARNER, D. S.      (DANNY)      EEEE05EN     OFF
  900 900701 TAYLOR, C. A.       (CARY)      WEWE04EN
  910 900701 BECKWITH, C. S.  (CHARLIE)      WEWE05EN     OFF
  920 900701 MITCHELL, T. E.      (TED)      YTSS21EN
  930 900701 MCWILLIAMS, L. W. (LARRY)       YTDS20EN
  940 900701 WALLACE, C. R.    (CURTIS)      WEWE12EN
  950 900701 JOHNSON, M. O.      (MARK)      WLWL01EN     OFF
  960 900701 THORNTON, L. D.    (LARRY)      SSSS02EN
  970 900701 ROSS, R. N.       (RONNIE)      YTSS40EN
  980 900701 QUILLEN, M. K.      (MIKE)      SSSS01EN
```

ENTER=INQ/RSTRT PF3=EXIT PF4=SENIORITY MOVE PF7=UP PF8=DN
PRESS PFKEY8 TO SEE MORE
                         SENIORITY ROSTER INQUIRY
   ROSTER CODE: AB   EMP-NBR: DIST: SDIST:
              ROSTER DESCRIPTION: MEMPHIS DIST ROAD CONDR
                                            ASGNMENT   STATUS
  X RANK   DATE   EMPLOYEE NAME
     990 900701 HALLMARK, R. H.   (HARLON)   EEEEO4EN
    1000 900701 ADAY, R. JR.   (RAYMOND) DLDL89EN
    1010 900701 PHILLIPS, S. R.   (STEVE)   MCMCO1EN
    1020 900701 WINCHESTER, A. C. (ARTHUR)   MCMCO9EN
    1030 900701 WRIGHT, P. D.   (PHILLIP) MCMCO3EN
    1040 900701 COOK, P. E.   (PAUL)   YTDS40EN
    1050 900701 COLLINSWORTH, S. E.(STEVE)   EX0001EN
    1060 900701 LIVINGSTON, A. D. (DIXON)   EEEEO1EN
    1070 900701 MALONE, R. G.   (RANDY)   MCMCO2EN
    1080 900701 PACE, T. R.   (TONY)   MCMC14EN
    1090 900701 DAVIS, G. L.   (GARY)   OFF
    1100 900701 CROWE, P. W.   (PHILLIP) MCMCO5EN
    1110 900701 MCANALLY, C. D.   (CHRIS)   EEEEO6EN   OFF
    1120 900701 BOATWRIGHT, G. E. (GEORGE)   EEEEO3EN
    1130 900701 CHEATHAN, D.E.   PROMOTED
    1140 900701 HOLLANDER, D. T.   (DANNY)   MCMC10EN
    1150 900701 HILL, M. W.   (MIKE)   NANAO6ET
    1160 900701 WAGNON, T. R.   (TIM)   MCMCO6EN
  ENTER=INQ/RSTRT PF3=EXIT PF4=SENIORITY MOVE PF7=UP PF8=DN
  PRESS PFKEY8 TO SEE MORE
                         SENIORITY ROSTER INQUIRY
   ROSTER CODE: AB   EMP-NBR: DIST: SDIST:
              ROSTER DESCRIPTION: MEMPHIS DIST ROAD CONDR
                                            ASGNMENT   STATUS
  X RANK   DATE   EMPLOYEE NAME
    1170 900701 ALEXANDER, B. N.   (BN)   JLJL91EN
    1190 900701 SIMS, J. L.   (JIMMY)   JLJL90EN
    1200 900701 ROGERS, R. W.   (WAYNE)   JLJL92EN   VACATIO
    1210 900701 DELOACH, H. S.   (HARRY)   EX0001E2   OFF
    1220 900701 BARNETT, A. B.   (BUCK)   EX0002E2
    1230 900701 KELLEY, R. D.   (RICKY)   WLWLO2EN   OFF
    1240 900701 BROWN, M. H. II   (HUGH)   EEEEO2EN   TO-PLAC
    1250 900701 GOOCH, G. K.   (KENNY)   MCMC13EN
    1260 900701 STEEN, R. M.   (RONALD)   MCMC15EN
    1270 900701 ASKEW, J. M.   (JIMMY)   NANAO2EN
    1280 900701 BARKER, D. D.   (DANNY)   PLPLO1EN
    1290 900701 HAMM, J. G.   DISABLED
    1300 900701 OLIVE, W. K.   (WENDEL)   NANAO8EN
    1310 900701 JOHNSON, L.   (LEO)   NANAO6EN
    1320 900701 HAWKINS, H. C.   PROMOTED
    1330 900701 CARTER, J. J.   DISABLED
    1350 900701 WALLACE, W. E.   PROMOTED
    1360 900701 PICKETT, D. L.   (DANNY)   NANAO4EN
  ENTER=INQ/RSTRT PF3=EXIT PF4=SENIORITY MOVE PF7=UP PF8=DN
  PRESS PFKEY8 TO SEE MORE

```
                    SENIORITY ROSTER INQUIRY
      ROSTER CODE: AB   EMP-NBR:            DIST:      SDIST:
           ROSTER DESCRIPTION: MEMPHIS DIST ROAD CONDR
   <  RANK    DATE        EMPLOYEE NAME           ASGNMENT      STATUS
      1370 900701 STAFFORD, L. M.      (DOC)       EX0017E6
      1380 900701 WAID, J. D.                      PROMOTED
      1390 900701 THORNTON, D. A.      (DAVE)      SHSH01EN
      1400 900701 FUTRELL, L. M.       (PETE)      NANA03EN
      1410 900701 FLANAGAN, G. N.      (GREG)      EX0002E6
      1420 900701 DAVIDSON, S. M.   (STEPHEN)      MCMC11EN
      1430 900701 WORSHAM, M. E.       (MIKE)      EX0005E6
      1440 900701 BADGETT, J. L.      (JOHNNY)     EX0001E6
      1450 900701 BALENTINE, J. R.                 EX0032E6
      1460 900701 GOODWIN, B. J. (BOBBY JOE)       EX0023E6
      1470 910605 MAYFIELD, J. L.      (JEFF)      EX0008E1
      1475 910606 COOK, M. JR          (MILTON)    DLDL89C0
      1480 911212 COLGLAZIER, A. K.    (ALAN)      EX0029E6
      1490 920102 MOORE, C. L.         (CLAYTON)   CTCT95B1
      1500 920102 WILLINGHAM, N. D.    (NEAL)      SSSS01B1
      1510 920102 BROOKS, W. E.                    DISABLED    OFF
      1520 920102 COOK, M. L.          (MIKE)      WLWL01B1
      1530 920102 ROBBINS, H. R.     DISABLED      DISABLED    OFF
   ENTER=INQ/RSTRT  PF3=EXIT  PF4=SENIORITY MOVE  PF7=UP   PF8=DN
   PRESS PFKEY8 TO SEE MORE
                    SENIORITY ROSTER INQUIRY
      ROSTER CODE: AB   EMP-NBR:            DIST:      SDIST:
           ROSTER DESCRIPTION: MEMPHIS DIST ROAD CONDR
   X  RANK    DATE        EMPLOYEE NAME           ASGNMENT      STATUS
      1540 920102 MCKINNEY, G. D.      (DAVID)     ELEL42B1
      1550 920102 SIZEMORE, R. H.      (ROY)       SSSS02B1
      1560 920102 BATES, P. W.         (PHILLIP)   EX0003B1
      1570 920102 DEAN, T. R.          (RAY)       EX0001B1
      1580 920102 PEGRAM, W. O.        (WENDELL)   YTFS01F0
      1590 920102 HESTER, F. A.        (FREDDIE)   YTSS05F0
      1600 920102 UNDERWOOD, E. A.     (ERNEST)                OFF
      1610 920102 VANDIVER, N. A.      (ABE)       YTSS01F0
      1620 920102 HOLT, J. C.          (JC)        DISABLED    OFF
      1640 920102 TUSCH, D. M.         (DAVID)     YTFS01S1
      1650 920102 HOBSON, L. E.        (LE)        EEEE02C0
      1660 920102 HARPER, H.           (HEAVY)     XTFS60F0
      1680 920102 BECHARD, E. B. JR (ERNEST)       YTSS02F0
      1700 920102 PITTMAN, W. E.       (WILLIE)    MCMC16C0
      1710 920102 PAINTER, J. B. JR    (JIM)       OFFICIAL
      1720 920102 HIGGINS, C. R.     DISABLED      DISABLED    OFF
      1730 920102 ROBERSON, F. L.      (FREDDIE)   OFFICIAL
      1740 920102 CARTER, T. R. JR     (TR)                    OFF
   ENTER=INQ/RSTRT  PF3=EXIT  PF4=SENIORITY MOVE  PF7=UP   PF8=DN  P
   PRESS PFKEY8 TO SEE MORE
```

SENIORITY ROSTER INQUIRY
ROSTER CODE: AB   EMP-NBR: DIST: SDIST:
ROSTER DESCRIPTION: MEMPHIS DIST ROAD CONDR

X	RANK	DATE	EMPLOYEE NAME		ASGNMENT	STATUS
	1750	920102	HARRIS, J. E. JR	(JIM)	YTSS02S1	
	1760	920102	MALONE, C. W.	(BUZZ)	YTSS41FO	
	1770	920102	MILLER, P. B. JR	(PERCY)	EX0009C1	
	1780	920102	PARKER, B. P.	(BOYD)	YTSS41S1	
	1790	920102	MCCLURE, S. R.	(SAM)	YTSS20FO	
	1800	920102	MYHAN, M. R.	(MELVIN)	EX0004C1	
	1830	920102	CARLTON, J. W.	(JAMES)	YTFY20YA	
	1840	920102	BOX, J. C.	(JC)	YTSS01S1	
	1850	920102	KIMBROUGH, L. T.	(TRUMAN)	YTSS40FO	OFF
	1860	920102	DALRYMPLE, L. D.	(LARRY)	YTSS05S1	
	1870	920102	KRIEGER, W. A.	(WILLIAM)	YTSS21FO	
	1880	920102	BOMPREZZI, H.	(HAROLD)		OFF
	1890	920102	PACE, J. H.	(JACKIE)	XTSS61S1	
	1900	920102	PACE, R. J.	(RAYBURN)	XTSS61FO	
	1920	920102	COPELAND, N. D.	(DALE)	YTSS21S1	
	1930	920102	POWELL, G. W.	(GARY)	YTSS20S1	
	1940	920102	STANLEY, J.	(JIMMY)	XTSS62S1	
	1950	920102	RICHARDSON, R. A.	(RICKY)	YTDS01FO	

ENTER=INQ/RSTRT   PF3=EXIT   PF4=SENIORITY MOVE   PF7=UP   PF8=DN   F
PRESS PFKEY8 TO SEE MORE

SENIORITY ROSTER INQUIRY
ROSTER CODE: AB   EMP-NBR: DIST: SDIST:
ROSTER DESCRIPTION: MEMPHIS DIST ROAD CONDR

X	RANK	DATE	EMPLOYEE NAME		ASGNMENT	STATUS
	1960	920102	HOWARD, J. W.	(BUTCH)	XTSS62FO	
	1970	920102	WATTS, R. H.	(RODA)		OFF
	1980	920102	CUNNINGHAM, J. F.	(JOHN)	XTDS60FO	VACATION
	1990	920102	RHODES, S. E.	(STEVE)	MCMC12EN	
	2000	920102	WRIGHT, D. W.	(DALE)	YTSS40S1	
	2030	920102	RHODES, J. D.	(JD)	EX0005SW	
	2040	920102	PUTNAM, C. L.	(CURTIS)	YTDS40FO	
	2050	920102	CLEMENT, R. E.	(GENE)	YTDS40S1	OFF
	2060	920102	VANDIVER, C. P.		DISABLED	
	2070	920102	DIXON, L. D.	(LARRY)	MCMC16EN	
	2080	920102	BURT, N.	(NATE)	YTFS40S1	
	2090	920102	CONWAY, T. L. JR	(TROY)	EX0009E1	
	2100	920102	PATE, E. R.	(EDDIE)	YTSY30YA	
	2110	920102	FLANAGAN, S. B.	(STEVE)	YTDS01S1	
	2120	920102	FULLER, J. P.	(PAT)	XTDS60S1	
	2130	920102	BAGGETT, A. K.	(KEN)	YTDS20FO	
	2140	920102	JAMES, L. R.	DISABLED	DISABLED	OFF
	2160	920102	LOWERY, T. D.	(TYRONE)	EX0006SW	

ENTER=INQ/RSTRT   PF3=EXIT   PF4=SENIORITY MOVE   PF7=UP   PF8=DN   PF
PRESS PFKEY8 TO SEE MORE

```
                    SENIORITY ROSTER INQUIRY
     ROSTER CODE: AB   EMP-NBR:            DIST:      SDIST:
              ROSTER DESCRIPTION: MEMPHIS DIST ROAD CONDR
  X   RANK    DATE        EMPLOYEE NAME          ASGNMENT     STATUS
     2170 920102 PATE, P. D.          (PAUL)     EX0006C1
     2180 920102 GOODMAN, M. W.       (MIKE)     EEEE04C0
     2190 920102 KIDD, L. W.          (LELAND)   EX0001SW     OFF
     2200 920102 DIRMEYER, P. H. JR   (PHIL)     EX0011C1     OFF
     2210 920102 ROGERS, M. E.        (MICKEY)   EX0011B1     OFF
     2220 920102 HAYNES, J. E.        (JIM)      DLDL89B1
     2230 920102 JENKINS, E. N.       (ED)       YTDS20S1
     2240 920102 FRAZIER, A. W.       (TONY)     EEEE03C0
     2250 920102 OAKLEY, J. III       (JACK)     EX0003C1
     2260 920102 EPPS, P. JR          (PHILMOR)  YTFY01YA
     2270 920102 JOHNSON, C. E.       (CHARLES)  YTFS40F0
     2280 920102 BARNES, E. L.        (LEON)                  OFF
     2290 920102 WALKER, E. L.        (ERIC)     EX0004E1
     2300 920102 ABERNATHY, G. R.     (GEORGE)   EX0011E1
     2310 920102 SMITH, T. D.         (TERRY)    EX0021E1     OFF
     2320 920102 ANDERSON, S. D.      (STEVE)    EX0022E1
     2330 920102 MASHBURN, T. O.      (TIM)      EX0023E1
     2340 920102 MALONE, M. Q.        (MIKE)     EX0020E1
 ENTER=INQ/RSTRT  PF3=EXIT  PF4=SENIORITY MOVE  PF7=UP  PF8=DN
 PRESS PFKEY8 TO SEE MORE
                    SENIORITY ROSTER INQUIRY
     ROSTER CODE: AB   EMP-NBR:            DIST:      SDIST:
              ROSTER DESCRIPTION: MEMPHIS DIST ROAD CONDR
  X   RANK    DATE        EMPLOYEE NAME          ASGNMENT     STATUS
     2350 920102 CURTIS, J. R.        (RANDY)    EX0007C1
     2360 920102 KENT, T. H.          (TIM)      EX0043C1     VACATION
     2370 920102 SCOTT, R. D.         (RONALD)   EX0041C1
     2380 920102 ONEILL, L. D.        (DEWAYNE)  EX0038C1
     2390 920102 MURPHY, P. D.        (PHILLIP)  EX0036C1
     2400 920102 OAKLEY, B. L.                   EX0042C1
     2410 920102 MYRICK, S. K.        (STEVE)    YTFY40YA     OFF
     2420 931119 GUNNIN, G. T.        (TODD)     EX0046C1
     2430 931119 ADDERHOLD, G. D.                EX0040C1
     2440 931119 SELLERS, C. M.       (MATT)     EX0002SW
     2450 940201 MCBRIDE, A. W.       (ALLEN)    EX0013C1
     2460 940527 WILSON, E. H.        (EDWARD)   YTFS20EN
     2470 940527 LILES, K. D.         (KENNY)    EX0010SW
     2500 940922 KIRK, P. D.          (PHILLIP)  YTFS20S1
     2510 940922 BAUGHN, J. T.        (TIM)      EX0045C1
     2520 940922 MASON, B. L.         (BILL)                  TO-PLACE
     2550 940922 WILSON, C. M.        (CHRIS)    EX0012C1
     2560 940922 ELLEDGE, C. A.       (ANDY)     EX0011SW
 ENTER=INQ/RSTRT  PF3=EXIT  PF4=SENIORITY MOVE  PF7=UP  PF8=DN  I
 PRESS PFKEY8 TO SEE MORE
```

```
    2590 940922 HOLT, P. W.        (WAYNE)    XTFS60S1              TN   SR
    2620 960202 SCOGGINS, G. A.    (GREG)     UNQUAL      OFF      TN   TN
    2640 960202 SIZEMORE, J. T.    (TODD)     EEEE05ET             TN   SR
    2650 960202 FRANKS, M. B.      (MATT)     MCMC06ET             TN   SR
    2670 961111 CARTER, K. D.    (KENNETH)    MCMC11ET             TN   SR
ENTER=INQ/RSTRT PF1=HELP PF3=EXIT PF4=SEN MOVE PF7=UP PF8=DN PF11=PREV MENU
PRESS PFKEY8 TO SEE MORE
                    SENIORITY ROSTER INQUIRY                     PSTS02F
   ROSTER CODE: AB   EMP-NBR:          DIST:      SDIST:    SERVICE:
              ROSTER DESCRIPTION: MEMPHIS DIST ROAD CONDR
 X  RANK   DATE       EMPLOYEE NAME        ASGNMENT    STATUS   DIST/SDIST
    2680 961111 PENDLEY, D. W.    (DAVID)    MCMC08ET             TN   SR
    2690 970628 CLARK, T. S.     (THOMAS)    EX0020C1             TN   SR
    2700 970628 MANSELL, J. R.    (JAMES)    EX0017C1             TN   SR
    2710 970628 MASHBURN, T. F.   (TERRY)    EX0010C1             TN   SR
    2720 970628 PENDLEY, C. D.  (CHARLES)    EX0018C1             TN   SR
    2730 970628 DEVANEY, J. M.    (JASON)    EX0014C1             TN   SR
    2740 970628 ADDERHOLD, B. L.   (BRAD)    EX0004C1             TN   SR
    2760 970628 MCALPIN, R. E.   (RODNEY)    EX0047C1             TN   SR
    2780 970628 HALL, L. J.       (LARRY)    EX0013SW             TN   SR
    2790 970628 MALONE, H. B.   (BRADLEY)    YTFS20FO    OFF      TN   SR
    2800 980617 CURTIS, M. R.    (MARCUS)    EX0003B1             TN   SR
    2810 980617 OLIVER, K. W.   (KENNETH)    YTFS20S1             TN   SR
    2820 980617 OLIVE, JR., W. K.  (KEITH)               OFF      TN   TN
    2830 980806 UTLEY, J. M.    (JEREMEY)    EX0011S1             TN   SR
    2350 981012 LONGMIRE, R. E.   (RICKY)              TO-PLACE   TN   SR
    2360 981012 GARRETT, D. F.    (DAVID)    YTDS40CT             TN   SR
    2370 981012 CREASY, S. W.   (STEPHEN)    WLWL02CT             TN   SR
    2390 981012 BRYAN, J. B.    (JEFFREY)    YTDS20CT             TN   SR
    2440 981012 MCCULLOCH, M. A.  (MYRON)    EEEE03CT             TN   SR
    2520 981019 COOK, M. A.       (MARK)                          TN   SR
    2530 981019 MALONE, C. B.    (BRENT)     WEWE10CT             TN   SR
    2630 981019 BREWER, P. D.  (PHILLIP)     WEWE03CT             TN   SR
    2640 981019 BURNS, B. T.     (TOMMY)                          TN   SR
    2650 981019 CARTER, R. S.   (RONNIE)     YTDS01CT             TN   SR
    2690 981019 HUTCHINS, J. J.    (JOE)     WEWE04CT             TN   SR
    4810 980928 SEAL, S. N.      (SHAWN)     ELEL42CT             TN   SR
   41704 980921 SPRINGER, C. B.             WLWL01CT             TN   SR
   41823 800619 YOUNG, W. C.      (CHAD)                OFF      TN   SR
   41994 980921 GRISHAM, J. O.              YTSS01CT             TN   SR
   42023 980921 WILLIS, D. M.               EEEE09CT             TN   SR
   42178 980921 HAYES, J. H.                EEEE01CT             TN   SR
   42306 980928 WILLINGHAM, J. P.           DLDL89CT             TN   SR
ENTER=INQ/RSTRT PF1=HELP PF3=EXIT PF4=SEN MOVE PF7=UP PF8=DN PF11=PREV MENU
PRESS PFKEY8 TO SEE MORE
                    SENIORITY ROSTER INQUIRY                     PSTS02F
   ROSTER CODE: CT   EMP-NBR:          DIST: TN  SDIST: SR  SERVICE:
              ROSTER DESCRIPTION: ALL DIV'S COND. TRAINEES*
 X  RANK   DATE       EMPLOYEE NAME        ASGNMENT    STATUS   DIST/SDIST
   42308 980921 RIDGEWAY, D. R.             EEEE07CT             TN   SR
  134333 981026 OLIVER, W. K.  (WILLIAM)                         TN   SR
  889972 981026 COAN, B. W.     (BRYAN)     WEWE01CT             TN   SR
```

Page 1 - Road Engineers

```
                    SENIORITY ROSTER INQUIRY                    PSTS02F
     ROSTER CODE: AF   EMP-NBR:        DIST:     SDIST:     SERVICE:
             ROSTER DESCRIPTION: MEMPHIS DIST RD ENGINEERS
 X   RANK   DATE       EMPLOYEE NAME        ASGNMENT   STATUS    DIST/SDIST
      10 710701 HAYNES, E. E.       (ED)     WEWE08EN            TN   SR
      20 710821 PUTNAM, B. G.       (BILLY)  ELEL42EN            TN   SR
      30 711218 CLARK, R. L.        (RONNIE) WEWE01EN  VACATION  TN   SR
      40 720916 HINTON, P. M.       (PAUL)   YTSS41EN            TN   SR
      50 730314 HUTTON, W. D.       (WILLIE) WEWE11EN            TN   SR
      60 730314 MURPHY, W. C.       (WC)     WEWE06EN            TN   SR
      70 730314 ELLIOTT, R. G.      (RAYMOND) WEWE03EN           TN   SR
      80 760427 PATTERSON, H. R.    (PAT)    WEWE09EN            TN   SR
     100 760806 ELLEDGE, S. E.      (SAM)    CTCT95EN            TN   SR
     120 770201 RILEY, B. E.        (BRAD)   YTSS01EN            TN   SR
     130 770201 PORTER, G. A.       (AL.)    YTFS01EN            TN   SR
     140 770201 BLAYLOCK, J. D.     (JOHN)   YTSS02EN            TN   SR
     150 770201 OLIVIS, J. W.       (JERRY)  YTSS20EN  VACATION  TN   SR
     160 770201 ZABRISKY, J. C.     (JOHN)   YTSS05EN            TN   SR
     170 770201 FARRIS, G. H.       (GLENDON) YTDS01EN           TN   SR
     180 770201 WALKER, J. E.       (JOHNNY) XTSS61EN  VACATION  TN   SR
     190 770201 MAYES, A. JR.       (ALFRED) XTFS60EN            TN   SR
     200 770206 GARNER, D. S.       (DANNY)  EEEE05EN  OFF       TN   SR
 ENTER=INQ/RSTRT  PF3=EXIT  PF4=SENIORITY MOVE  PF7=UP  PF8=DN  PF11=PREV MENU
 PRESS PFKEY8 TO SEE MORE
                    SENIORITY ROSTER INQUIRY                    PSTS02F
     ROSTER CODE: AF   EMP-NBR:        DIST:     SDIST:     SERVICE:
             ROSTER DESCRIPTION: MEMPHIS DIST RD ENGINEERS
 X   RANK   DATE       EMPLOYEE NAME        ASGNMENT   STATUS    DIST/SDIST
     210 770207 TAYLOR, C. A.       (CARY)   WEWE04EN            TN   SR
     220 770317 BECKWITH, C. S.  (CHARLIE)   WEWE05EN    off     TN   SR
     230 770317 MITCHELL, T. E.     (TED)    YTSS21EN            TN   SR
     240 770317 MCWILLIAMS, L. W.   (LARRY)  YTDS20EN  VACATION  TN   SR
     250 780825 WALLACE, C. R.      (CURTIS) WEWE12EN            TN   SR
     260 781101 JOHNSON, M. O.      (MARK)   WLWL01EN            TN   SR
     270 781214 THORNTON, L. D.     (LARRY)  SSSS02EN            TN   SR
     280 790503 YOUNG, C. F. JR.    (SMOOTH) WEWE02EN            TN   SR
     290 790507 ROSS, R. N.         (RONNIE) YTSS40EN            TN   SR
     300 790508 QUILLEN, M. K.      (MIKE)   SSSS01EN            TN   SR
     310 790509 CLEMONS, A. L.      (AL.)    WEWE10EN            TN   SR
     320 790510 HALLMARK, R. H.     (HARLON) MCMC05EN            TN   SR
     330 790511 UTLEY, W. G.        (GARY)   MCMC02EN            TN   SR
     340 790618 UNDERWOOD, L. K.    (LANCE)  XTDS60EN            TN   SR
     350 790720 ADAY, R. JR.        (RAYMOND) DLDL89EN           TN   SR
     360 791017 PHILLIPS, S. R.     (STEVE)  MCMC01EN            TN   SR
     370 791018 MYHAN, M. E.        (MIKE)   XTSS62EN            TN   SR
     380 791019 WINCHESTER, A. C. (ARTHUR)   MCMC09EN            TN   SR
 ENTER=INQ/RSTRT  PF3=EXIT  PF4=SENIORITY MOVE  PF7=UP  PF8=DN  PF11=PREV MENU
 PRESS PFKEY8 TO SEE MORE
```

Page 2 - Road Engineers

```
                    SENIORITY ROSTER INQUIRY                    PSTS02F
     ROSTER CODE: AF    EMP-NBR:          DIST:    SDIST:    SERVICE:
              ROSTER DESCRIPTION: MEMPHIS DIST RD ENGINEERS
  X   RANK    DATE       EMPLOYEE NAME        ASGNMENT    STATUS    DIST/SDIST
      390 791020 WRIGHT, P. D.     (PHILLIP)  MCMC03EN              TN   SR
      400 800219 COOK, P. E.       (PAUL)     YTDS40EN              TN   SR
      410 800226 COLLINSWORTH, S. E.(STEVE)   EX0001EN   VACATION   TN   SR
      420 800229 LIVINGSTON, A. D. (DIXON)    EEEE01EN   VACATION   TN   SR
      430 800411 MALONE, R. G.     (RANDY)    WEWE07EN              TN   SR
      440 800723 PACE, T. R.       (TONY)     EEEE03EN              TN   SR
      450 801020 DAVIS, G. L.      (GARY)                OFF        TN   TN
      460 801021 CROWE, P. W.      (PHILLIP)  EEEE04EN              TN   SR
      470 801202 MCANALLY, C. D.   (CHRIS)    EEEE06EN              TN   SR
      480 810528 BOATWRIGHT, G. E. (GEORGE)   EEEE02EN              TN   SR
      490 810714 SMITHERS, N. B.   (NICK)     YTFS40EN              TN   SR
      500 810714 CHEATHAN, D.E.               OFFICIAL              TN   TN
      510 810714 HOLLANDER, D. T.  (DANNY)    MCMC10EN              TN   SR
      520 810717 HILL, M. W.       (MIKE)     MCMC08EN              TN   SR
      530 810717 WAGNON, T. R.     (TIM)      MCMC06EN              TN   SR
      540 880628 ALEXANDER, B. N.  (BN)       JLJL91EN              TN   SR
      560 880628 SIMS, J. L.       (JIMMY)    JLJL90EN              TN   SR
      570 880628 ROGERS, R. W.     (WAYNE)    JLJL92EN   OFF        TN   SR
  ENTER=INQ/RSTRT   PF3=EXIT  PF4=SENIORITY MOVE   PF7=UP   PF8=DN  PF11=PREV MENU
  PRESS PFKEY8 TO SEE MORE
                    SENIORITY ROSTER INQUIRY                    PSTS02F
     ROSTER CODE: AF    EMP-NBR:          DIST:    SDIST:    SERVICE:
              ROSTER DESCRIPTION: MEMPHIS DIST RD ENGINEERS
  X   RANK    DATE       EMPLOYEE NAME        ASGNMENT    STATUS    DIST/SDIST
      580 880628 DELOACH, H. S.    (HARRY)    EX0001E2              TN   SR
      590 880628 BARNETT, A. B.    (BUCK)     EX0002E2   VACATION   TN   SR
      600 880628 KELLEY, R. D.     (RICKY)    WLWL02EN              TN   SR
      610 881031 BROWN, M. H. II   (HUGH)     EX0012E1              TN   SR
      620 881031 GOOCH, G. K.      (KENNY)    MCMC13EN              TN   SR
      630 881031 STEEN, R. M.      (RONALD)   EX0002E1              TN   SR
      640 881101 ASKEW, J. M.      (JIMMY)    NANA02EN              AL   ME
      650 881101 BARKER, D. D.     (DANNY)    PLPL01EN              AL   ME
      660 881101 HAMM, J. G.                  DISABLED              AL   AL
      670 881101 OLIVE, W. K.      (WENDEL)   NANA01EN              AL   ME
      680 881101 JOHNSON, L.       (LEO)      NANA03EN   VACATION   AL   ME
      690 881101 HAWKINS, H. C.               PROMOTED              AL   AL
      700 881101 CARTER, J. J.                DISABLED              AL   AL
      720 881101 WALLACE, W. E.               PROMOTED              AL   AL
      730 881101 PICKETT, D. L.    (DANNY)    NANA08EN   OFF        AL   ME
      740 881101 STAFFORD, L. M.   (DOC)      EX0017E6   OFF        AL   ME
      750 881101 WAID, J. D.                  PROMOTED              AL   AL
      760 881101 THORNTON, D. A.   (DAVE)     SHSH01EN              AL   ME
  ENTER=INQ/RSTRT   PF3=EXIT  PF4=SENIORITY MOVE   PF7=UP   PF8=DN  PF11=PREV MENU
  PRESS PFKEY8 TO SEE MORE
```

Page 3 - Road Engineers

```
                    SENIORITY ROSTER INQUIRY                    PSTS02F
     ROSTER CODE: AF   EMP-NBR:        DIST:      SDIST:      SERVICE:
              ROSTER DESCRIPTION: MEMPHIS DIST RD ENGINEERS
  X   RANK    DATE        EMPLOYEE NAME          ASGNMENT    STATUS    DIST/SDIST
      770 881101 FUTRELL, L. M.      (PETE)      NANA06EN              AL   ME
      780 881101 FLANAGAN, G. N.     (GREG)      NANA04EN              AL   ME
      790 881101 DAVIDSON, S. M.     (STEPHEN)   MCMC11EN              TN   SR
      800 881101 WORSHAM, M. E.      (MIKE)      EX0005E6              AL   ME
      810 881101 BADGETT, J. L.      (JOHNNY)    EX0001E6              AL   ME
      820 881101 BALENTINE, J. R.                EX0021E6              AL   ME
      830 881101 GOODWIN, B. J.  (BOBBY JOE)     EX0012E6              AL   ME
      840 911210 BYRD, D.            (DARNELL)   MCMC04EN              TN   SR
      850 911210 HUDSON, J. S.       (STEVE)     MCMC07EN              TN   SR
      860 920104 COLGLAZIER, A. K.   (ALAN)      EX0029E6              AL   ME
      880 930325 HUBBERT, P. L.      (PAUL)      EX0030E6   VACATION   AL   ME
      890 930716 RHODES, S. E.       (STEVE)     MCMC12EN              TN   SR
      900 930806 DIXON, L. D.        (LARRY)     EX0007E1              TN   SR
      910 931029 WEEKS, D. L.        (DANNY)     EX0031E6              AL   ME
      920 931029 MILLS, R. C.        (RONALD)    EX0005E1              TN   SR
      930 931029 MAYFIELD, J. L.     (JEFF)      EX0008E1              TN   SR
      940 931029 MICHAEL, A. D.      (DALE)      EX0031E1              TN   SR
      950 931029 CONWAY, T. L. JR    (TROY)      EX0009E1              TN   SR
  ENTER=INQ/RSTRT  PF3=EXIT  PF4=SENIORITY MOVE  PF7=UP  PF8=DN  PF11=PREV MENU
  PRESS PFKEY8 TO SEE MORE
                    SENIORITY ROSTER INQUIRY                    PSTS02F
     ROSTER CODE: AF   EMP-NBR:        DIST:      SDIST:      SERVICE:
              ROSTER DESCRIPTION: MEMPHIS DIST RD ENGINEERS
  X   RANK    DATE        EMPLOYEE NAME          ASGNMENT    STATUS    DIST/SDIST
      960 931126 LANDERS, J. H. JR   (JACK)      EX0030E1   VACATION   TN   SR
      970 931126 HAND, D. J.         (DON)       EX0006E1   VACATION   TN   SR
      980 931126 RICKARD, C. A.      (ALAN)      EX0013E6              AL   ME
      990 940410 HILL, G. A.         (GREG)      EX0022E6   VACATION   AL   ME
     1000 940520 THOMPSON, T. R.     (TY)        EX0010E1              TN   SR
     1010 940726 WALKER, E. L.       (ERIC)      EX0015E1              TN   SR
     1020 940726 ABERNATHY, G. R.    (GEORGE)    EX0011E1              TN   SR
     1030 940726 SMITH, T. D.        (TERRY)     EX0013E1              TN   SR
     1040 940726 ANDERSON, S. D.     (STEVE)     EX0003E1              TN   SR
     1050 940726 MASHBURN, T. O.     (TIM)       EX0004E1              TN   SR
     1060 940726 MALONE, M. Q.       (MIKE)      EX0001E1   OFF        TN   SR
     1070 940726 CURTIS, J. R.       (RANDY)     EX0019E1              TN   SR
     1080 941212 KENT, T. H.         (TIM)       EX0018E1              TN   SR
     1090 950317 SCOTT, R. D.        (RONALD)    EX0024C1              TN   SR
     1100 950317 ONEILL, L. D.       (DEWAYNE)   EX0007C1              TN   SR
     1110 950317 MURPHY, P. D.       (PHILLIP)   EX0027C1              TN   SR
     1120 950317 OAKLEY, B. L.                   EX0001C1              TN   SR
     1130 951030 GUNNIN, G. T.       (TODD)      EX0005C1              TN   SR
  ENTER=INQ/RSTRT  PF3=EXIT  PF4=SENIORITY MOVE  PF7=UP  PF8=DN  PF11=PREV MENU
  PRESS PFKEY8 TO SEE MORE
```

Page 4 - Road Engineers

```
                    SENIORITY ROSTER INQUIRY                 PSTS02F
     ROSTER CODE: AF    EMP-NBR:        DIST:     SDIST:    SERVICE:
                ROSTER DESCRIPTION: MEMPHIS DIST RD ENGINEERS
X   RANK   DATE      EMPLOYEE NAME           ASGNMENT    STATUS    DIST/SDIST
    1140 951031 BEARD, T. E.        (TOMMY)  EX0003C6              AL   ME
    1150 951031 ADDERHOLD, G. D.             EX0028C1              TN   SR
    1160 960524 SELLERS, C. M.      (MATT)   XTFS60S1              TN   SR
    1170 961021 MCBRIDE, A. W.      (ALLEN)  EX0008C1              TN   SR
    1180 961021 WILSON, E. H.       (EDWARD) EX0011SW              TN   SR
    1190 961021 LILES, K. D.        (KENNY)  EX0009SW              TN   SR
    1220 970414 BAUGHN, J. T.       (TIM)    EX0017C1              TN   SR
```

```
ENTER=INQ/RSTRT  PF3=EXIT  PF4=SENIORITY MOVE  PF7=UP  PF8=DN  PF11=PREV MENU
END OF ROSTER
```

Page 1 - Yard Engineers

```
                    SENIORITY ROSTER INQUIRY                    PSTS02F
     ROSTER CODE: AH    EMP-NBR:          DIST:      SDIST:      SERVICE:
               ROSTER DESCRIPTION: MEMPHIS DIST YARD ENGRS
   X  RANK    DATE        EMPLOYEE NAME          ASGNMENT      STATUS    DIST/SDIST
      20  681208 RILEY, B. E.         (BRAD)    YTSS01EN                 TN    SR
      30  690405 PORTER, G. A.        (AL)      YTFS01EN    VACATION     TN    SR
      40  690427 BLAYLOCK, J. D.      (JOHN)    YTSS02EN    VACATION     TN    SR
      50  710123 OLIVIS, J. W.        (JERRY)   YTSS20EN                 TN    SR
      60  710501 ZABRISKY, J. C.      (JOHN)    YTSS05EN                 TN    SR
      70  710520 FARRIS, G. H.      (GLENDON)   YTDS01EN                 TN    SR
      80  720630 WALKER, J. E.        (JOHNNY)  XTSS61EN                 TN    SR
      90  740702 MAYES, A. JR.        (ALFRED)  XTFS60EN                 TN    SR
     100  770201 HAYNES, E. E.        (ED)      WEWE08EN                 TN    SR
     110  770201 PUTNAM, B. G.        (BILLY)   ELEL42EN                 TN    SR
     120  711218 CLARK, R. L.         (RONNIE)  WEWE01EN                 TN    SR
     130  770201 HINTON, P. M.        (PAUL)    YTSS41EN                 TN    SR
     140  770317 MITCHELL, T. E.      (TED)     YTSS21EN                 TN    SR
     150  770317 MCWILLIAMS, L. W.   (LARRY)    YTDS20EN                 TN    SR
     160  780825 WALLACE, C. R.       (CURTIS)  WEWE12EN    VACATION     TN    SR
     170  781101 JOHNSON, M. O.       (MARK)    WLWL01EN                 TN    SR
     180  781214 THORNTON, L. D.      (LARRY)   SSSS02EN                 TN    SR
     190  790503 YOUNG, C. F. JR.     (SMOOTH)  WEWE02EN                 TN    SR
   ENTER=INQ/RSTRT   PF3=EXIT   PF4=SENIORITY MOVE   PF7=UP   PF8=DN   PF11=PREV MENU
   PRESS PFKEY8 TO SEE MORE
                    SENIORITY ROSTER INQUIRY                    PSTS02F
     ROSTER CODE: AH    EMP-NBR:          DIST:      SDIST:      SERVICE:
               ROSTER DESCRIPTION: MEMPHIS DIST YARD ENGRS
   X  RANK    DATE        EMPLOYEE NAME          ASGNMENT      STATUS    DIST/SDIST
     200  790507 ROSS, R. N.          (RONNIE)  YTSS40EN                 TN    SR
     210  790508 QUILLEN, M. K.       (MIKE)    SSSS01EN                 TN    SR
     220  790509 CLEMONS, A. L.       (AL)      WEWE10EN                 TN    SR
     230  790510 HALLMARK, R. H.      (HARLON)  MCMC05EN                 TN    SR
     240  790511 UTLEY, W. G.         (GARY)    MCMC02EN    VACATION     TN    SR
     250  790618 UNDERWOOD, L. K.     (LANCE)   XTDS60EN                 TN    SR
     260  790720 ADAY, R. JR.         (RAYMOND) DLDL89EN                 TN    SR
     270  791017 PHILLIPS, S. R.      (STEVE)   MCMC01EN                 TN    SR
     280  791018 MYHAN, M. E.         (MIKE)    XTSS62EN                 TN    SR
     290  791019 WINCHESTER, A. C. (ARTHUR)     MCMC09EN                 TN    SR
     300  791020 WRIGHT, P. D.        (PHILLIP) MCMC03EN                 TN    SR
     310  800219 COOK, P. E.          (PAUL)    YTDS40EN                 TN    SR
     320  800226 COLLINSWORTH, S. E.(STEVE)     EX0001EN                 TN    SR
     330  800229 LIVINGSTON, A. D.    (DIXON)   EEEE01EN                 TN    SR
     340  800411 MALONE, R. G.        (RANDY)   WEWE07EN    OFF          TN    SR
     350  800723 PACE, T. R.          (TONY)    EEEE03EN                 TN    SR
     360  801020 DAVIS, G. L.         (GARY)                OFF          TN    TN
     370  801021 CROWE, P. W.         (PHILLIP) EEEE04EN                 TN    SR
   ENTER=INQ/RSTRT   PF3=EXIT   PF4=SENIORITY MOVE   PF7=UP   PF8=DN   PF11=PREV MENU
   PRESS PFKEY8 TO SEE MORE
```

Page 2 - Yard Engineers

```
                    SENIORITY ROSTER INQUIRY                      PSTS02F
     ROSTER CODE: AH    EMP-NBR:           DIST:     SDIST:     SERVICE:
               ROSTER DESCRIPTION: MEMPHIS DIST YARD ENGRS
 X   RANK   DATE       EMPLOYEE NAME          ASGNMENT   STATUS    DIST/SDIST
                                                                    TN    SR
     380 801202 MCANALLY, C. D.    (CHRIS)   EEEE06EN                TN    SR
     390 810528 BOATWRIGHT, G. E. (GEORGE)   EEEE02EN                TN    SR
     400 810714 SMITHERS, N. B.     (NICK)   YTFS40EN                TN    SR
     410 810714 CHEATHAN, D.E.               OFFICIAL               TN    TN
     420 810714 HOLLANDER, D. T.   (DANNY)   MCMC10EN  VACATION      TN    SR
     430 810717 HILL, M. W.         (MIKE)   MCMC08EN                TN    SR
     440 810717 WAGNON, T. R.        (TIM)   MCMC06EN                TN    SR
     450 880628 ALEXANDER, B. N.      (BN)   JLJL91EN                TN    SR
     470 880628 SIMS, J. L.        (JIMMY)   JLJL90EN                TN    SR
     480 880628 ROGERS, R. W.      (WAYNE)   JLJL92EN  OFF           TN    SR
     490 880628 DELOACH, H. S.     (HARRY)   EX0001E2  OFF           TN    SR
     500 880628 BARNETT, A. B.      (BUCK)   EX0002E2                TN    SR
     510 880628 KELLEY, R. D.      (RICKY)   WLWL02EN                TN    SR
     520 881031 BROWN, M. H. II     (HUGH)   EX0012E1                TN    SR
     530 881031 GOOCH, G. K.       (KENNY)   MCMC13EN                TN    SR
     540 881031 STEEN, R. M.      (RONALD)   EX0002E1                TN    SR
     550 881101 ASKEW, J. M.       (JIMMY)   NANA02EN                AL    ME
     560 881101 BARKER, D. D.      (DANNY)   PLPL01EN                AL    ME
 ENTER=INQ/RSTRT  PF3=EXIT  PF4=SENIORITY MOVE  PF7=UP  PF8=DN  PF11=PREV MENU
 PRESS PFKEY8 TO SEE MORE
```

```
                    SENIORITY ROSTER INQUIRY                      PSTS02F
     ROSTER CODE: AH    EMP-NBR:           DIST:     SDIST:     SERVICE:
               ROSTER DESCRIPTION: MEMPHIS DIST YARD ENGRS
 X   RANK   DATE       EMPLOYEE NAME          ASGNMENT   STATUS    DIST/SDIST
     570 881101 HAMM, J. G.                  DISABLED               AL    AL
     580 881101 OLIVE, W. K.      (WENDEL)   NANA01EN               AL    ME
     590 881101 JOHNSON, L.          (LEO)   NANA03EN  OFF          AL    ME
     600 881101 HAWKINS, H. C.               PROMOTED               AL    AL
     610 881101 CARTER, J. J.                DISABLED               AL    AL
     630 881101 WALLACE, W. E.               PROMOTED               AL    AL
     640 881101 PICKETT, D. L.     (DANNY)   NANA08EN               AL    ME
     650 881101 STAFFORD, L. M.      (DOC)   EX0017E6               AL    ME
     660 881101 WAID, J. D.                  PROMOTED               AL    AL
     670 881101 THORNTON, D. A.     (DAVE)   SHSH01EN               AL    ME
     680 881101 FUTRELL, L. M.      (PETE)   NANA06EN               AL    ME
     690 881101 FLANAGAN, G. N.     (GREG)   NANA04EN               AL    ME
     700 881101 DAVIDSON, S. M.  (STEPHEN)   MCMC11EN               TN    SR
     710 881101 WORSHAM, M. E.      (MIKE)   EX0005E6               AL    ME
     720 881101 BADGETT, J. L.    (JOHNNY)   EX0001E6               AL    ME
     730 881101 BALENTINE, J. R.             EX0021E6               AL    ME
     740 881101 GOODWIN, B. J. (BOBBY JOE)   EX0012E6               AL    ME
     750 911210 BYRD, D.         (DARNELL)   MCMC04EN               TN    SR
 ENTER=INQ/RSTRT  PF3=EXIT  PF4=SENIORITY MOVE  PF7=UP  PF8=DN  PF11=PREV MENU
 PRESS PFKEY8 TO SEE MORE
```

Page 3 - Yard Engineers

```
                        SENIORITY ROSTER INQUIRY                    PSTS02F
       ROSTER CODE: AH   EMP-NBR:          DIST:      SDIST:     SERVICE:
                ROSTER DESCRIPTION: MEMPHIS DIST YARD ENGRS
   X   RANK    DATE        EMPLOYEE NAME         ASGNMENT     STATUS     DIST/SDIST
       760  911210  HUDSON, J. S.      (STEVE)   MCMC07EN                 TN   SR
       770  920104  COLGLAZIER, A. K.  (ALAN)    EX0029E6                 AL   ME
       790  930325  HUBBERT, P. L.     (PAUL)    EX0030E6                 AL   ME
       800  930716  RHODES, S. E.      (STEVE)   MCMC12EN                 TN   SR
       810  930806  DIXON, L. D.       (LARRY)   EX0007E1                 TN   SR
       820  931029  WEEKS, D. L.       (DANNY)   EX0031E6                 AL   ME
       830  931029  MILLS, R. C.       (RONALD)  EX0005E1                 TN   SR
       840  931029  MAYFIELD, J. L.    (JEFF)    EX0008E1                 TN   SR
       850  931029  MICHAEL, A. D.     (DALE)    EX0031E1                 TN   SR
       860  931029  CONWAY, T. L. JR   (TROY)    EX0009E1                 TN   SR
       870  931126  LANDERS, J. H. JR  (JACK)    EX0030E1     OFF         TN   SR
       880  931126  HAND, D. J.        (DON)     EX0006E1                 TN   SR
       890  931126  RICKARD, C. A.     (ALAN)    EX0013E6                 AL   ME
       900  940410  HILL, G. A.        (GREG)    EX0022E6                 AL   ME
       910  940520  THOMPSON, T. R.    (TY)      EX0010E1                 TN   SR
       920  940726  WALKER, E. L.      (ERIC)    EX0015E1     VACATION    TN   SR
       930  940726  ABERNATHY, G. R.   (GEORGE)  EX0011E1     OFF         TN   SR
       940  940726  SMITH, T. D.       (TERRY)   EX0013E1     OFF         TN   SR
   ENTER=INQ/RSTRT  PF3=EXIT  PF4=SENIORITY MOVE  PF7=UP  PF8=DN  PF11=PREV MENU
   PRESS PFKEY8 TO SEE MORE
                        SENIORITY ROSTER INQUIRY                    PSTS02F
       ROSTER CODE: AH   EMP-NBR:          DIST:      SDIST:     SERVICE:
                ROSTER DESCRIPTION: MEMPHIS DIST YARD ENGRS
   X   RANK    DATE        EMPLOYEE NAME         ASGNMENT     STATUS     DIST/SDIST
       950  940726  ANDERSON, S. D.    (STEVE)   EX0003E1                 TN   SR
       960  940726  MASHBURN, T. O.    (TIM)     EX0004E1                 TN   SR
       970  940726  MALONE, M. Q.      (MIKE)    EX0001E1                 TN   SR
       980  940726  CURTIS, J. R.      (RANDY)   EX0019E1                 TN   SR
       990  941212  KENT, T. H.        (TIM)     EX0018E1                 TN   SR
      1000  950317  SCOTT, R. D.       (RONALD)  EX0024C1     VACATION    TN   SR
      1010  950317  ONEILL, L. D.      (DEWAYNE) EX0007C1                 TN   SR
      1020  950317  MURPHY, P. D.      (PHILLIP) EX0027C1                 TN   SR
      1030  950317  OAKLEY, B. L.                EX0001C1                 TN   SR
      1040  951030  GUNNIN, G. T.      (TODD)    EX0005C1                 TN   SR
      1050  951031  BEARD, T. E.       (TOMMY)   EX0003C6                 AL   ME
      1060  951031  ADDERHOLD, G. D.             EX0028C1     VACATION    TN   SR
      1070  960524  SELLERS, C. M.     (MATT)    XTFS60S1                 TN   SR
      1080  961021  MCBRIDE, A. W.     (ALLEN)   EX0008C1     OFF         TN   SR
      1090  961021  WILSON, E. H.      (EDWARD)  EX0011SW                 TN   SR
      1100  961021  LILES, K. D.       (KENNY)   EX0009SW     OFF         TN   SR

   ENTER=INQ/RSTRT  PF3=EXIT  PF4=SENIORITY MOVE  PF7=UP  PF8=DN  PF11=PREV MENU
   END OF ROSTER
```

Page 1 - Yard Foremen

SENIORITY ROSTER INQUIRY   PSTS02F
ROSTER CODE: AD EMP-NBR: DIST: SDIST: SERVICE:
ROSTER DESCRIPTION: MEMPHIS DIST YD FOREMEN

X	RANK	DATE	EMPLOYEE NAME		ASGNMENT	STATUS	DIST/SDIST	
	10	591120	PEGRAM, W. O.	(WENDELL)	YTFS01FO		TN	SR
	20	600121	HESTER, F. A.	(FREDDIE)	YTSS05FO		TN	SR
	30	600211	UNDERWOOD, E. A.	(ERNEST)		OFF	TN	TN
	40	600224	VANDIVER, N. A.	(ABE)	YTSS01FO		TN	SR
	50	600224	HOLT, J. C.	(JC)	YTSS02FO	OFF	TN	SR
	60	600320	BROWN, J. L.	(JAMES)		OFF	TN	TN
	70	600518	TUSCH, D. M.	(DAVID)	YTFS01S1	VACATION	TN	SR
	80	600525	HOBSON, L. E.	(LE)		TO-PLACE	TN	SR
	90	621027	HARPER, H.	(HEAVY)	XTFS60FO		TN	SR
	100	630122	WARDLOW, D. R.	(DALE)		OFF	TN	TN
	110	630625	BECHARD, E. B. JR	(ERNEST)	YTSS20FO		TN	SR
	130	640829	PITTMAN, W. E.	(WILLIE)	EX0009C1		TN	SR
	140	640829	PAINTER, J. B. JR	(JIM)	OFFICIAL		TN	TN
	150	640829	HIGGINS, C. R. DISABLED		DISABLED	OFF	TN	XX
	160	640829	ROBERSON, F. L.	(FREDDIE)	OFFICIAL		TN	TN
	170	651231	CARTER, T. R. JR	(TR)	YTSS21FO	OFF	TN	SR
	180	651231	HARRIS, J. E. JR	(JIM)	YTSS02S1	OFF	TN	SR
	190	660228	MALONE, C. W.	(BUZZ)	YTSS41FO		TN	SR

ENTER=INQ/RSTRT PF3=EXIT PF4=SENIORITY MOVE PF7=UP PF8=DN PF11=PREV MENU
PRESS PFKEY8 TO SEE MORE

SENIORITY ROSTER INQUIRY   PSTS02F
ROSTER CODE: AD EMP-NBR: DIST: SDIST: SERVICE:
ROSTER DESCRIPTION: MEMPHIS DIST YD FOREMEN

X	RANK	DATE	EMPLOYEE NAME		ASGNMENT	STATUS	DIST/SDIST	
	200	660813	MILLER, P. B. JR	(PERCY)	EX0016C1		TN	SR
	210	661008	PARKER, B. P.	(BOYD)	YTSS41S1		TN	SR
	220	661008	EPPS, P. JR	(PHILMOR)	YTFY01YA		TN	YD
	230	670826	MCCLURE, S. R.	(SAM)	XTSS61FO		TN	SR
	240	680210	MYHAN, M. R.	(MELVIN)	EX0004C1		TN	SR
	250	680420	ROSS, R. N.	(RONNIE)	YTSS40EN		TN	SR
	280	690108	CARLTON, J. W.				TN	TN
	290	690410	BOX, J. C.	(JC)	YTSS01S1	VACATION	TN	SR
	300	690428	KIMBROUGH, L. T.	(TRUMAN)	YTSS40FO		TN	SR
	320	691206	JOHNSON, C. E.	(CHARLES)	YTFS40FO		TN	SR
	330	700106	WILLIS, B. J. DISABLED		DISABLED	TO-PLACE	TN	XX
	340	700302	DALRYMPLE, L. D.	(LARRY)	YTSS05S1		TN	SR
	350	700508	KRIEGER, W. A.	(WILLIAM)	YTSS21S1		TN	SR
	360	701030	BOMPREZZI, H.	(HAROLD)		OFF	TN	SR
	370	710204	PACE, J. H.	(JACKIE)	XTSS61S1		TN	SR
	380	710507	PACE, R. J.	(RAYBURN)	XTSS62FO		TN	SR
	390	711021	PITTS, J. A.	(JIM)	XTSS62S1	OFF	TN	SR
	400	720315	COPELAND, N. D.	(DALE)	YTDS01FO		TN	SR

ENTER=INQ/RSTRT PF3=EXIT PF4=SENIORITY MOVE PF7=UP PF8=DN PF11=PREV MENU
PRESS PFKEY8 TO SEE MORE

Page 2 - Yard Foremen

SENIORITY ROSTER INQUIRY   PSTS02F
ROSTER CODE: AD   EMP-NBR: DIST: SDIST: SERVICE:
ROSTER DESCRIPTION: MEMPHIS DIST YD FOREMEN

X	RANK	DATE	EMPLOYEE NAME		ASGNMENT	STATUS	DIST/SDIST	
	410	720316	POWELL, G. W.	(GARY)	YTSS20S1	VACATION	TN	SR
	420	720420	STANLEY, J.	(JIMMY)	YTSS40S1		TN	SR
	430	720701	RICHARDSON, R. A.	(RICKY)	YTDS01S1		TN	SR
	440	720824	HOWARD, J. W.	(BUTCH)	EX0010SW		TN	SR
	450	720824	WATTS, R. H.	(RODIE)	YTDS40FO	OFF	TN	SR
	460	730722	CREASY, J. P.	(PAUL)	WEWE06CO	VACATION	TN	SR
	470	730722	BENNETT, J. E.	(JAMES)	WEWE01CO		TN	SR
	490	730722	MOORE, C. L.	(CLAYTON)	CTCT95B1		TN	SR
	500	730722	WILLINGHAM, N. D.	(NEAL)	SSSS01B1	OFF	TN	SR
	510	730722	KILPATRICK, J. C.	(PAT)	WEWE08CO	OFF	TN	SR
	520	730722	FLEMING, J. D.	(JD)	WEWE03CO		TN	SR
	530	730722	GRISHAM, L. E.	(LUTHER)	WEWE09CO		TN	SR
	540	730722	BROOKS, W. E.	DISABLED	DISABLED	OFF	TN	TN
	550	730722	JACKSON, R. M.	(MIKE)	WEWE04CO		TN	SR
	560	730722	GRISHAM, B. G.	(BOBBY)	WEWE10CO		TN	SR
	570	730722	COOK, M. L.	(MIKE)	WLWL01B1		TN	SR
	590	730722	MICHAEL, A. D.	(DALE)	EX0031E1		TN	SR
	600	730722	ROBBINS, H. R.	DISABLED	DISABLED	OFF	TN	TN

ENTER=INQ/RSTRT PF3=EXIT PF4=SENIORITY MOVE PF7=UP PF8=DN PF11=PREV MENU
PRESS PFKEY8 TO SEE MORE

SENIORITY ROSTER INQUIRY   PSTS02F
ROSTER CODE: AD   EMP-NBR: DIST: SDIST: SERVICE:
ROSTER DESCRIPTION: MEMPHIS DIST YD FOREMEN

X	RANK	DATE	EMPLOYEE NAME		ASGNMENT	STATUS	DIST/SDIST	
	610	730722	MCKINNEY, G. D.	(DAVID)	ELEL42B1		TN	SR
	630	730722	JORDAN, T. D.	(DAVID)	MCMC05CO		TN	SR
	640	730722	SIZEMORE, R. H.	(ROY)	SSSS02B1		TN	SR
	650	730722	BATES, P. W.	(PHILLIP)	EX0003B1		TN	SR
	660	730722	DEAN, T. R.	(RAY)	EX0012SW		TN	SR
	670	731006	QUILLEN, M. K.	(MIKE)	SSSS01EN		TN	SR
	680	731010	CUNNINGHAM, J. F.	(JOHN)	XTDS60FO	VACATION	TN	SR
	690	731011	RHODES, S. E.	(STEVE)	MCMC12EN		TN	SR
	700	731012	WRIGHT, D. W.	(DALE)	YTDS20FO		TN	SR
	710	731103	BYRD, W. T.	DISABLED	DISABLED	OFF	TN	XX
	720	731103	UTLEY, W. G.	(GARY)	MCMC02EN	VACATION	TN	SR
	740	740702	RHODES, J. D.	(JD)	EX0005SW		TN	SR
	750	750901	CLEMONS, A. L.	(AL)	WEWE10EN		TN	SR
	760	760110	PHILLIPS, S. R.	(STEVE)	MCMC01EN		TN	SR
	770	760110	HALLMARK, R. H.	(HARLON)	MCMC05EN		TN	SR
	780	760110	PUTNAM, C. L.	(CURTIS)	YTDS40S1		TN	SR
	790	760403	POPE, G. S.	(STEVE)	ELEL42CO		TN	SR
	800	760408	LARIMORE, J.	(JIMMY)	SSSS01CO		TN	SR

ENTER=INQ/RSTRT PF3=EXIT PF4=SENIORITY MOVE PF7=UP PF8=DN PF11=PREV MENU
PRESS PFKEY8 TO SEE MORE

Page 3 - Yard Foremen

```
                    SENIORITY ROSTER INQUIRY                    PSTS02F
      ROSTER CODE: AD   EMP-NBR:          DIST:      SDIST:     SERVICE:
               ROSTER DESCRIPTION: MEMPHIS DIST YD FOREMEN
   X   RANK    DATE        EMPLOYEE NAME          ASGNMENT    STATUS    DIST/SDIST
       810 760409 UNDERWOOD, L. K.    (LANCE)     XTDS60EN               TN    SR
       820 760409 CLEMENT, R. E.      (GENE)      EX0004SW               TN    SR
       830 760417 SMITH, W. D.        (DALE)      SSSS02CO               TN    SR
       840 760418 VANDIVER, C. P.                 DISABLED              TN    TN
       850 760418 DIXON, L. D.        (LARRY)     EX0007E1               TN    SR
       860 760522 HESTER, D. A.       (DON)       WLWL01CO               TN    SR
       870 760522 MYHAN, M. E.        (MIKE)      XTSS62EN               TN    SR
       880 760605 BURT, N.            (NATE)      YTFS40S1               TN    SR
       890 761207 SOFTLY, W. A.       (WILLIAM)   CTCT95CO               TN    SR
       900 761214 CONWAY, T. L. JR    (TROY)      EX0009E1               TN    SR
       910 761219 ADAY, R. JR.        (RAYMOND)   DLDL89EN               TN    SR
       920 770120 PATE, E. R.         (EDDIE)     YTSY30YA               TN    YD
       930 770225 WINCHESTER, A. C. (ARTHUR)      MCMC09EN               TN    SR
       940 770225 FLANAGAN, S. B.     (STEVE)     YTDS20S1               TN    SR
       950 770513 BYRD, D.            (DARNELL)   MCMC04EN               TN    SR
       960 770513 WRIGHT, P. D.       (PHILLIP)   MCMC03EN               TN    SR
       970 770611 FULLER, J. P.       (PAT)       XTDS60S1               TN    SR
       980 770613 BAGGETT, A. K.      (KEN)       DLDL89B1               TN    SR
   ENTER=INQ/RSTRT   PF3=EXIT   PF4=SENIORITY MOVE   PF7=UP   PF8=DN   PF11=PREV MENU
   PRESS PFKEY8 TO SEE MORE
                    SENIORITY ROSTER INQUIRY                    PSTS02F
      ROSTER CODE: AD   EMP-NBR:          DIST:      SDIST:     SERVICE:
               ROSTER DESCRIPTION: MEMPHIS DIST YD FOREMEN
   X   RANK    DATE        EMPLOYEE NAME          ASGNMENT    STATUS    DIST/SDIST
       990 780126 JAMES, L. R.        DISABLED    DISABLED    OFF       TN    XX
      1000 780126 COOK, P. E.         (PAUL)      YTDS40EN               TN    SR
      1010 780406 COLLINSWORTH, S. E.(STEVE)      EX0001EN               TN    SR
      1020 780406 LIVINGSTON, A. D.   (DIXON)     EEEE01EN               TN    SR
      1030 780406 MALONE, R. G.       (RANDY)     WEWE07EN    OFF        TN    SR
      1040 780406 WADE, J. C.         (CLIFF)     WEWE05CO               TN    SR
      1050 780406 PACE, T. R.         (TONY)      EEEE03EN               TN    SR
      1060 780411 COOK, M. JR         (MILTON)    DLDL89CO               TN    SR
      1070 780710 CASTLEBERRY, S. L.  (STEVE)     MCMC08CO    OFF        TN    SR
      1080 780710 ACKLIN, L. E. SR.   (LEWIS)     MCMC04ET               TN    SR
      1090 780710 LOWERY, T. D.       (TYRONE)    EX0006SW               TN    SR
      1100 780710 CROWE, G. F.        (GREG)      MCMC07CO    OFF        TN    SR
      1110 780710 GRISHAM, B. D.                                         TN    TN
      1120 780710 SOUTHERN, C. S.     (STEVE)     WEWE07CO    OFF        TN    SR
      1130 780710 DUGGER, T. W.       (TOM)       EEEE01CO               TN    SR
      1140 780804 BOATWRIGHT, G. E. (GEORGE)      EEEE02EN               TN    SR
      1150 780804 PATE, P. D.         (PAUL)      EX0006C1               TN    SR
      1160 780804 GOODMAN, M. W.      (MIKE)      EEEE04CO               TN    SR
   ENTER=INQ/RSTRT   PF3=EXIT   PF4=SENIORITY MOVE   PF7=UP   PF8=DN   PF11=PREV MENU
   PRESS PFKEY8 TO SEE MORE
```

Page 4 - Yard Foremen

```
                    SENIORITY ROSTER INQUIRY                    PSTS02F
     ROSTER CODE: AD   EMP-NBR:        DIST:      SDIST:     SERVICE:
               ROSTER DESCRIPTION: MEMPHIS DIST YD FOREMEN
  X  RANK   DATE        EMPLOYEE NAME          ASGNMENT    STATUS    DIST/SDIST
     1170 780804 DAVIS, G. L.        (GARY)                  OFF     TN   TN
     1180 780804 CROWE, P. W.        (PHILLIP)   EEEE04EN            TN   SR
     1190 780804 RICHARDSON, L. L. (LANDEL)                  OFF     TN   SR
     1200 780804 KIDD, L. W.         (LELAND)    EX0001SW            TN   SR
     1210 781027 MANSELL, R. K.      (RANDY)     WEWE02CO            TN   YD
     1220 781027 GARDNER, D. N.      (DANNY)     MCMC01CO            TN   SR
     1230 781027 MCANALLY, C. D.     (CHRIS)     EEEE06EN            TN   SR
     1240 781027 DIRMEYER, P. H. JR  (PHIL)      EX0011C1   OFF      TN   SR
     1250 790203 PICKERING, G. S.    (STEVE)     MCMC02CO            TN   SR
     1260 790203 ALBRIGHT, T. W.     (TED)       MCMC10CO            TN   SR
     1370 790203 SMITHERS, N. B.     (NICK)      YTFS40EN            TN   SR
     1280 790203 ROGERS, M. E.       (MICKEY)               OFF      TN   SR
     1290 790203 BEARD, T. W.        (TIM)       MCMC06CO            TN   SR
     1300 790203 HAYNES, J. E.       (JIM)       EX0002B1            TN   SR
     1310 790311 WILLIS, J. M.       (JOE)       MCMC13CO            TN   SR
     1320 790312 MARTIN, W. E.       (WILLIE)    MCMC09CO            TN   SR
     1330 790612 MANSELL, L. G.      (LARRY)     MCMC11CO            TN   SR
     1340 790612 LANDERS, J. H. JR   (JACK)      EX0030E1   OFF      TN   SR
  ENTER=INQ/RSTRT  PF3=EXIT  PF4=SENIORITY MOVE  PF7=UP  PF8=DN  PF11=PREV MENU
  PRESS PFKEY8 TO SEE MORE
```

```
                    SENIORITY ROSTER INQUIRY                    PSTS02F
     ROSTER CODE: AD   EMP-NBR:        DIST:      SDIST:     SERVICE:
               ROSTER DESCRIPTION: MEMPHIS DIST YD FOREMEN
  X  RANK   DATE        EMPLOYEE NAME          ASGNMENT    STATUS    DIST/SDIST
```
```
     1350 790615 HAND, D. J.        (DON)       EX0006E1            TN   SR
     1360 790615 CAPERTON, K. D.    (DAMIEN)    EEEE05CO            TN   SR
     1370 790615 CHEATHAN, D.E.                 OFFICIAL           TN   TN
     1380 790803 REAVES, J. L.      (JAMES)                OFF     TN   SR
     1390 790803 JENKINS, E. N.     (ED)        EX0002SW   VACATION TN   SR
     1400 790803 HUDSON, J. S.      (STEVE)     MCMC07EN            TN   SR
     1410 790803 WARHURST, M. D.    (MIKE)      MCMC03CO            TN   SR
     1420 790827 SCHELL, T. R.      (TIM)       EEEE06CO   OFF      TN   SR
     1430 790827 HOLLANDER, D. T.   (DANNY)     MCMC10EN   VACATION TN   SR
     1440 790827 HILL, M. W.        (MIKE)      MCMC08EN            TN   SR
     1450 790827 WAGNON, T. R.      (TIM)       MCMC06EN            TN   SR
     1460 790829 BROWN, M. H. II    (HUGH)      EX0012E1            TN   SR
     1470 790829 DIXON, E. B.       (ED)                   OFF      TN   TN
     1480 790829 AGEE, R. J.        (RICK)      EX0026C1            TN   SR
     1490 800118 MOULTRIE, R. R.    (RICKY)     EEEE03CO            TN   SR
     1500 800118 GOOCH, G. K.       (KENNY)     MCMC13EN            TN   SR
     1510 800118 FRAZIER, A. W.     (TONY)      EEEE02CO            TN   SR
     1520 800322 MILLS, R. C.       (RONALD)    EX0005E1            TN   SR
  ENTER=INQ/RSTRT  PF3=EXIT  PF4=SENIORITY MOVE  PF7=UP  PF8=DN  PF11=PREV MENU
  PRESS PFKEY8 TO SEE MORE
```

Page 5 - Yard Foremen

```
                    SENIORITY ROSTER INQUIRY                    PSTS02F
   ROSTER CODE: AD    EMP-NBR:          DIST:      SDIST:     SERVICE:
              ROSTER DESCRIPTION: MEMPHIS DIST YD FOREMEN
 X   RANK   DATE       EMPLOYEE NAME         ASGNMENT    STATUS    DIST/SDIST
    1530 800322 MAYFIELD, J. L.     (JEFF)    EX0008E1              TN   SR
    1540 800402 OAKLEY, J. III      (JACK)    EX0003C1              TN   SR
    1550 800410 STEEN, R. M.        (RONALD)  EX0002E1              TN   SR
    1570 851101 RILEY, B. E.        (BRAD)    YTSS01EN              TN   SR
    1580 851101 PORTER, G. A.       (AL)      YTFS01EN   VACATION   TN   SR
    1590 851101 PATTERSON, H. R.    (PAT)     WEWE09EN   VACATION   TN   SR
    1600 851101 BLAYLOCK, J. D.     (JOHN)    YTSS02EN   VACATION   TN   SR
    1610 851101 OLIVIS, J. W.       (JERRY)   YTSS20EN              TN   SR
    1620 851101 ZABRISKY, J. C.     (JOHN)    YTSS05EN              TN   SR
    1630 851101 FARRIS, G. H.       (GLENDON) YTDS01EN              TN   SR
    1640 851101 HAYNES, E. E.       (ED)      WEWE08EN              TN   SR
    1650 851101 PUTNAM, B. G.       (BILLY)   ELEL42EN              TN   SR
    1660 851101 CLARK, R. L.        (RONNIE)  WEWE01EN              TN   SR
    1670 851101 HINTON, P. M.       (PAUL)    YTSS41EN              TN   SR
    1690 851101 WALKER, J. E.       (JOHNNY)  XTSS61EN              TN   SR
    1700 851101 HUTTON, W. D.       (WILLIE)  WEWE11EN              TN   SR
    1710 851101 MURPHY, W. C.       (WC)      WEWE06EN              TN   SR
    1720 851101 ELLIOTT, R. G.      (RAYMOND) WEWE03EN              TN   SR
 ENTER=INQ/RSTRT   PF3=EXIT   PF4=SENIORITY MOVE   PF7=UP   PF8=DN   PF11=PREV MENU
 PRESS PFKEY8 TO SEE MORE
                    SENIORITY ROSTER INQUIRY                    PSTS02F
   ROSTER CODE: AD    EMP-NBR:          DIST:      SDIST:     SERVICE:
              ROSTER DESCRIPTION: MEMPHIS DIST YD FOREMEN
 X   RANK   DATE       EMPLOYEE NAME         ASGNMENT    STATUS    DIST/SDIST
    1730 851101 MAYES, A. JR.       (ALFRED)  XTFS60EN              TN   SR
    1740 851101 ELLEDGE, S. E.      (SAM)     CTCT95EN              TN   SR
    1750 851101 GARNER, D. S.       (DANNY)   EEEE05EN              TN   SR
    1760 851101 TAYLOR, C. A.       (CARY)    WEWE04EN              TN   SR
    1770 851101 BECKWITH, C. S. (CHARLIE)     WEWE05EN   off        TN   SR
    1780 851101 MITCHELL, T. E.     (TED)     YTSS21EN              TN   SR
    1790 851101 MCWILLIAMS, L. W.   (LARRY)   YTDS20EN              TN   SR
    1800 851101 WALLACE, C. R.      (CURTIS)  WEWE12EN   VACATION   TN   SR
    1810 851101 JOHNSON, M. O.      (MARK)    WLWL01EN              TN   SR
    1820 851101 THORNTON, L. D.     (LARRY)   SSSS02EN              TN   SR
    1830 851101 YOUNG, C. F. JR.    (SMOOTH)  WEWE02EN              TN   SR
    1850 880628 ALEXANDER, B. N.    (BN)      JLJL91EN              TN   SR
    1860 880628 STANSELL, E. M. SR (MOLLY)    JLJL92C0              TN   SR
    1880 880628 ARNETT, C. D.       (CHARLES) JLJL92B1              TN   SR
    1890 880628 SIMS, J. L.         (JIMMY)   JLJL90EN              TN   SR
    1900 880628 COLLINS, J. N.      (JIMMY)   EX0002C2              TN   SR
    1910 880628 ROGERS, R. W.       (WAYNE)   JLJL92EN   OFF        TN   SR
    1920 880628 DELOACH, H. S.      (HARRY)   EX0001E2   OFF        TN   SR
 ENTER=INQ/RSTRT   PF3=EXIT   PF4=SENIORITY MOVE   PF7=UP   PF8=DN   PF11=PREV MENU
 PRESS PFKEY8 TO SEE MORE
```

300

Page 6 - Yard Foremen

```
                      SENIORITY ROSTER INQUIRY                      PSTS02F
      ROSTER CODE: AD    EMP-NBR:          DIST:      SDIST:      SERVICE:
            ROSTER DESCRIPTION: MEMPHIS DIST YD FOREMEN
  X  RANK   DATE       EMPLOYEE NAME           ASGNMENT    STATUS    DIST/SDIST
     1930 880628 BARNES, E. L.      (LEON)                 OFF        TN   TN
     1940 880628 BARNETT, A. B.     (BUCK)     EX0002E2                TN   SR
     1950 880628 JONES, J. J.       (JJ)       WLWL02C0               TN   SR
     1960 880628 KELLEY, R. D.      (RICKY)    WLWL02EN               TN   SR
     1970 880628 RUSHING, R. H.     (RH)       JLJL91C0               TN   SR
     1980 880628 BEARD, B. S. JR.   (BENNY)    JLJL91B1               TN   SR
     1990 880628 STEGALL, D. R.     (DON)      EX0001C2               TN   SR
     2000 880628 COWART, T. U.      (TUCK)                 OFF        TN   TN
     2010 880628 BISHOP, J. M.      (MIKE)     JLJL90C0   VACATION    TN   SR
     2020 880628 KISER, L. W.       (LW)       JLJL90B1   VACATION    TN   SR
     2030 880628 SCOTT, R. L.       (ROBERT)   MCMC12C0   VACATION    TN   SR
     2040 880628 HOLLEY, C. T.                 DISABLED   OFF         TN   TN
     2050 880628 BERRY, W. A.       (WAYNE)    MCMC04C0   VACATION    TN   SR
     2060 880628 BERRY, J. M.       (MIKE)     WLWL02B1               TN   SR
     2070 880628 MOORE, B. E.       (BARRY)    EX0001B1               TN   SR
     2080 890628 THOMPSON, T. R.    (TY)       EX0010E1               TN   SR
     2090 890923 WALKER, E. L.      (ERIC)     EX0015E1   VACATION    TN   SR
     2100 901029 ABERNATHY, G. R.   (GEORGE)   EX0011E1   OFF         TN   SR
  ENTER=INQ/RSTRT  PF3=EXIT  PF4=SENIORITY MOVE  PF7=UP  PF8=DN  PF11=PREV MENU
  PRESS PFKEY8 TO SEE MORE
                      SENIORITY ROSTER INQUIRY                      PSTS02F
      ROSTER CODE: AD    EMP-NBR:          DIST:      SDIST:      SERVICE:
            ROSTER DESCRIPTION: MEMPHIS DIST YD FOREMEN
  X  RANK   DATE       EMPLOYEE NAME           ASGNMENT    STATUS    DIST/SDIST
     2110 901029 SMITH, T. D.       (TERRY)    EX0013E1   OFF         TN   SR
     2120 901029 ANDERSON, S. D.    (STEVE)    EX0003E1               TN   SR
     2130 901029 MASHBURN, T. O.    (TIM)      EX0004E1               TN   SR
     2140 901029 MALONE, M. Q.      (MIKE)     EX0001E1               TN   SR
     2150 901029 CURTIS, J. R.      (RANDY)    EX0019E1               TN   SR
     2160 901029 KENT, T. H.        (TIM)      EX0018E1               TN   SR
     2170 910603 SCOTT, R. D.       (RONALD)   EX0024C1   VACATION    TN   SR
     2180 910603 ONEILL, L. D.      (DEWAYNE)  EX0007C1               TN   SR
     2190 910603 MURPHY, P. D.      (PHILLIP)  EX0027C1               TN   SR
     2200 910603 OAKLEY, B. L.                 EX0001C1               TN   SR
     2210 910603 MYRICK, S. K.      (STEVE)    XTFY70YA               TN   YD
     2220 931119 GUNNIN, G. T.      (TODD)     EX0005C1               TN   SR
     2230 931119 ADDERHOLD, G. D.              EX0028C1   VACATION    TN   SR
     2240 931119 SELLERS, C. M.     (MATT)     XTFS60S1               TN   SR
     2250 940201 MCBRIDE, A. W.     (ALLEN)    EX0008C1   OFF         TN   SR
     2260 940527 WILSON, E. H.      (EDWARD)   EX0011SW               TN   SR
     2270 940527 LILES, K. D.       (KENNY)    EX0009SW   OFF         TN   SR
     2290 940527 HOSEY, E. B.       (ERIC)     CCCC05ET               GA   GN
  ENTER=INQ/RSTRT  PF3=EXIT  PF4=SENIORITY MOVE  PF7=UP  PF8=DN  PF11=PREV MENU
  PRESS PFKEY8 TO SEE MORE
```

SENIORITY ROSTER INQUIRY   PSTS02F
ROSTER CODE: AD   EMP-NBR: DIST: SDIST: SERVICE:
          ROSTER DESCRIPTION: MEMPHIS DIST YD FOREMEN
X RANK   DATE   EMPLOYEE NAME   ASGNMENT   STATUS   DIST/SDIST
   2300 940922 KIRK, P. D.   (PHILLIP)   EX0002C1   TN   SR
   2310 940922 BAUGHN, J. T.   (TIM)   EX0017C1   TN   SR
   2320 940922 MASON, B. L.   (BILL)   MCMC06ET   TN   SR
   2350 940922 WILSON, C. M.   (CHRIS)   ELEL42ET   OFF   TN   SR
   2360 940922 ELLEDGE, C. A.   (ANDY)   EEEE03ET   TN   SR
   2390 940922 HOLT, P. W.   (WAYNE)   YTSS02ET   OFF   TN   SR
   2420 960202 SCOGGINS, G. A.   (GREG)   OFF   TN   SR
   2440 960202 SIZEMORE, J. T.   (TODD)   EX0003SW   TN   SR
   2450 960202 FRANKS, M. B.   (MATT)   EX0007SW   TN   SR
   2660 961111 HAWKINS, R.   (ROBERT)   EX0001S1   TN   SR
   2670 961111 CARTER, K. D.   (KENNETH)   YTFS20F0   TN   SR
   2680 961111 PENDLEY, D. W.   (DAVID)   YTFS20S1   TN   SR

   2690 970628 Clark, T. S.   (Thomas)
   2700 970628 Mansell, J. R.   (James)
   2710 970628 Mashburn, T. F.   (Terry)
   2720 970628 Pendley, C. D.   (Charles)
   2730 970628 Devaney, J. M.   (Jason)
   2740 970628 Adderhold, B. L.   (Brad)
   2760 970628 McAlpin, R. E.   (Rodney)
   2780 970628 Hall, L. J.   (Larry)
   2790 970628 Malone, H. B.   (Hershel)

ABOUT THE EDITOR

JACK DANIEL

If anyone ever grew up with the railroad it was this fellow. He lived a couple hundred feet from the mainline of Southern Railway and a stone's throw from the depot at Cherokee, AL, which is on the line from Sheffield to Memphis. His mom used to say, "those steam powered trains that roared through town or stopped at the depot or in the siding, caught Jack's undivided attention at an early age; so early in fact he would have to stand on tiptoe to see out the window."

As time went on, his fascination increased. It became a ritual for him to be on the front porch to greet train crews with a wave of the hand in the daytime. He used a flashlight at night for the wave. The crews would always be over on his side to return the wave and the engineer would usually give a couple of short blows of the whistle as an answer to his signal. The passing of "The Tennessean" about 10:30 p.m. brought the days' activities to a close for Jack. If some westbound had gone "in-the-hole" for the streamliner, then that required a visit to the engine crew. A favorite memory of those visits was about the engineer letting him flash the headlight on and off as soon as No. 46 came into view. That let the eastbound know that the freight was in the clear and out of the way and No. 46 would whiz by going about seventy miles per hour. Rules and tradition of that day required second-class freight trains to be in the clear at least fifteen minutes for the first-class passenger trains.

The affection for railroading did not decline in Jack's teen years. In fact, he had cultivated so many friendships with the train crews that he hated to miss seeing and waving to them while he was at school. He struck a deal with his mom to take his place and wave to the crews in his absence. She rejected the deal but did compromise by limiting her participation to listening for engineer Albert Crawford's whistle call "whippoorwill." Then she responded with a substitute wave in Jack's absence. Engineers Leslie D. McKinney and Richard Burns had special ways of blowing a whistle to let Jack know they were coming, too.

When school was out in the afternoon and on Saturdays as well as during summer vacation, Jack found time to visit the depot to continue learning the details of running a depot. Agent Frank Monk patiently taught him the various duties. One enjoyable duty was to copy train orders from the dispatchers in Sheffield, AL and then hand them up to the passing trains with the old bamboo order hoops. Dispatcher Glen Bryan and chief dispatcher Buddy Thompson took a special interest in Jack's enthusiasm and encouraged him. They hinted about a possible future in train dispatching. In fact, Glen and Buddy convinced superintendent Charlie Chandler that Jack would make a good candidate to become the traveling operator to go along with a work train in 1945 in order to keep the train from delaying wartime traffic. This became his first railroad job. He also worked the operator's extra board.

Jack's dad owned and operated a service station in Cherokee and he became ill and incapacitated in 1946. Jack had to take over the operation of the business until about 1950. This seemed to put an end to his pursuing a railroad career. His parents, realizing that Jack had asthma, insisted that he get further education. He attended Florence State Teachers College, now University of North Alabama, and graduated with a degree in Business Administration.

His first job out of college after a brief stint in the army was with the Colbert County Board of Education as a business manager. He then married and moved to Tuscumbia, AL. He was later elected to two terms as Colbert County Tax Collector with offices in the Courthouse. He was offered a job in Memphis, TN with the Memphis City Schools. In 1971, he and family moved and he worked in the Division of Finance until retirement in 1992.

When people learn that he is a railroad enthusiast, they usually ask if he ever modeled toy trains. The stock answer was "no, I played with live trains." His hobby allowed him to be co-founder and first president of the Muscle Shoals Railroad Club in Sheffield and president of the Memphis Chapter of the National Railway Historical Society. He is presently serving as historian of the Memphis Chapter.

He and wife Martha have a son and three daughters and six grandchildren. He no longer lives near a railroad but does have pleasant memories; so many that he published his first book, "SOUTHERN RAILWAY:STEVENSON TO MEMPHIS," in 1996.

Someone said memories are like diamonds, they are forever, and there is no wrecking ball nor welders torch that can ever take that away from us. We know that memory can fade away in one's golden years. That is why Jack thought it was best to edit this, his second book, while his memory was still fairly good. He truly hopes that railroaders appreciate his work for preserving data and pictures for future generations. For you guys and gals who are on the internet, his e-mail address is <JacknBlack@aol.com>.

304

INDEX TO A PORTRAIT OF A PEOPLE

A

Abernathy, George R. 206, 244
Acklin, Lewis 151, 223
Aday, Jr.,Raymond 246
Adcock, Rick A. 261
Agee, Ricky J. 232
Adderhold, Glen D. 233
Albright, Ted W. 227
Anderson, Steve D. 207, 247
Ashby, Victor 123, 258
Ashley, H. W. 13
Askew, Jimmy 172, 173, 177

B

Badgett, Johnny 166
Baggett, Kent 250
Bailey, Audrey 256
Baker, Jack 258
Balentine, Bobby 160
Barnes, James 57
Bates, Phillip 237
Baughn, J. Tim 221
Beard, Tim 240
Beard, Tommy 169
Beckwith, Charlie 186
Bennett, James 137, 213
Berry, Clyde 53, 55
Berry, Mike 238
Berry, Wayne A. 229
Bishop, J. H. Ray 179
Bishop, J. Mike 233
Bistline, James 34
Black, Fred 34, 38
Boatwright, George E 189
Borden, Billy 254, 261
Brown, Lance 37
Brown, II., M. Hugh 198
Brown, Willard C. 179
Byrd, Darnell 200

C

Caperton, K. Damien 228
Carlise, Jim 39
Carpenter, Russell 92
Carter, Kenneth D. 235, 242
Castleberry, Steve L. 221
Chandler, Dr. John 59
Clark, Ronnie 181
Clark, Thomas S. 236

Claytor, W. Graham 56
Clem, E. H. 20
Clemons, Al L. 190
Clements, Gene 260
Collingsworth, Steve 121
Conway, Troy 203
Cook, Mike 239
Cook, Milton 253
Cook, Paul 260
Cooper, Anson 92
Copeland, Dale 250
Cothren, Jackson 11
Couch, Bernard 40
Counts, Sarah 58
Crawford, Albert H. 33, 41
Crawford, Robert 13
Creasy, J. Paul 213
Crowe, Phillip W. 161, 195, 243, 264
Cunningham, John F. 246
Curtis, J. Randy 204, 275
Cutler, Ralph 179

D

Dalyrymple, L. D. 125
Daniel, Jack 60, 64, 302
Daugherty, Donnie 170
Davidson, Stephen M. 199
Dean, Ray 237, 249, 260
Deloach, Harry S. 197
Devaney, Jason M. 236
Dillahunty, Arthur 46
Dixon, Billy 257
Dixon, Joseph Edgar 30
Dixon, Larry 201
Diremeyer, Phillip H. 224
Dolan, Jimmy 167
Dotson, J. D. 170
Dubois, Jim 46
Dudley, Hugh 60
Dugger, Tom W. 224

E

Edwards, Cecil 36, 38
Edwards, J. W., Sr. 12
Edwards, J. W., Jr. 12, 21, 36, 38, 39
Edwards, Jimmy Foster 22
Edwards, Lena Rebecca 12

(continued)

Elledge, Andy 209
Elledge, Sam E. 182
Elliott, Raymond G. 152, 184
Ennis, Lawrence 54
Eudy, Ron 175
Everett, Vester L. 42

F

Farris, Glendon 247
Fischer, Julius 46
Flannigan, Steve 249
Fleming, J. D. 214, 244
Franks, Matt B. 234, 239
Frazier, A. W. 230
Fuller, J. Pat 125, 248, 251
Futrell, Pete 178

G

Gardner, Danny N. 225
Garner, Danny S. 185
Garner, Charlie 178
Garrett, Hugh 165
Gibson, Eric N. 42
Goins, Edgar 64
Goldstein, Abe 11
Gooch, G. Kenny 150, 196
Goodman, Mike W. 223
Goodwin, Bobby Joe 199
Gribble, D. E. 57
Grisham, Bobby 216
Grisham, Luther E. 215
Gunnin, G. Todd 211

H

Hackworth, Joseph R 50
Hall, David 168
Hallmark, R. Harlon 191
Hamlet, Ed 11
Hand, J. Don 205
Hanlin, Henry 46
Hargett, Bovel 37
Harrisson, Clyde 11
Haynes, Ed 181
Haynes, Jim Ed 254
Hill, Mike W. 196
Hobson, L. E. 218
Holland, Melvin 33, 41
Hollander, Danny T. 194
Holt, Wayne 232
Huddleston, W. C. 42

Hudson, J. Steve 200
Hutton, Bill "Willie D." 160, 163, 262

I

Inman, E. H. 46

J

Jackson, Arthur 11
Jackson, M. Mike 215
Jenkins, Ed N. 252
Johnson, Chris 256
Johnson, Mark O. 187
Jones, J. J. 229
Jones, Shorty 171
Jones, Wm. Scott 45
Jordan, Dave 158, 161, 239, 264

K

Kelley, Ricky D. 197
Kennedy, Ray R. 42
Kent, Tim H. 210
Kidd, Leland W. 251
Kilpatrick, J. C. 163, 214 , 262
Kimbrough, Don 50
Kimbrough, L. T. 124
Kimbrough, Marvin 45
Kimbrough, Maynard 48, 55
Kimbrough, Truman 122
King, John 172, 173
King, Steve, 257
Kirk, Phillip D. 212
Kiser, Herman P. 31, 45, 83
Kiser, Larry W. 241

L

Landers, Jr., Jack H. 205, 242
Larimore, Jimmy 219
Laughlin, R. W. 33
Lehman, Gregg 255
Lemay, Roger 259
Lemay, R. B. 11
Liles, Kenny Dale 234, 252
Livingston, A. Dixon 193

M

McAnnlly, Chris D. 193
McBride, Allen W. 231
McCord, Bob 37

(continued)

McCorkle, Floyd 46
McCorkle, Roy E. 35, 37
McKinney, G. David 218
McWilliams, John Hubert 39
McWilliams, Larry W. 245
Mabry, John 60
Malone, C. W. 153
Malone, Mike Q. 151, 183, 263
Malone, Milton "Buddy" 263
Malone, Randy G. 194
Malone, Rusty 263
Malone, Steve 263
Mansell, Larry G. 222
Mansell, Randy 124, 238
Maples, Jim 37
Martin, Luther 11
Martin, William Earl 205, 227
Mashburn, Tim O. 208
Mayer, Dr. Raymond 57
Mayfield, Jeff L. 204
Meadows, Herbert R. 47
Michael, A. Dale 202
Middleton, Alice L. 55
Miller, Percy 202
Mills, Ronald C. 202
Mitchell, Ted 248
Mitchell, Will 11
Moore, Barry 229
Morgan, Russell 179
Morris, Tom 42
Moss, F. J. 60
Moultrie, Ricky 230, 240
Murphy, Phillip D. 212
Murphy, W. C. 183
Myhan, Melvyn Ray 156, 217

N

Naves, Tom 12
Nelson, Ernest 46
Nixon, Grady 58

O

Oakley, III, Jack 231
O'Neill, L. Dewayne 211
Osborn, O. O. 45

P

Pace, J. H. 122
Pace, Rayburn 159
Pace, Tony R. 195

Painter, J. B. 121
Pannell, Hyman 37
Pate, Paul D. 150, 222
Patterson, H. R. "Pat" 184
Pendley, Charles Douglas 224
Pendley, David W. 235
Phillips, Steve R. 192
Pickett, Danny 171
Pickering, Steve 196, 225
Pinkley, F. P. 23, 45, 50,
Pittman, Willie E. 217
Pope, G. Steve 219
Powell, Gary 259
Purdie, Bill 83
Putnam, Billy G. 182
Putnam, Curtis 260

Q

Quillen, Mike K. 189, 190

R

Ramsey, Eddie 170
Rea, John 56
Reed, J. C. 42
Rhodes, Steve E. 201
Rice, Paul 42
Richardson, Ricky 253
Ricks, Percy 37
Riley, Brad Eugene 151, 153
Robinson, Hugh L. 42
Rudd, Bill 57
Rudder, Vernon 38
Russell, James "Goat" 29

S

Sanders, Col. Harlan 34
Schafer, John 56
Schell, Tim R. 228
Scott, Robert L. 229
Scott, Ronald D. 210, 248
Sharp, Tommy 175
Shea, J. N. 11
Shelly, J. O. 11
Shields, Chester 57
Shrader, Dave 37
Sims, Herbert 64
Sims, Jim 60
Sizemore, Clyde 170
Sizemore, Roy 188

(continued)

Sizemore, Todd 238
Smith, Aubrey 55
Smith, Charles L. 60, 179
Smith, Terry D. 207
Smith, W. Dale 260
Sockwell, Denzil 55
Softly, William A. 220
Southern, Steve 221
Spencer, Jim 123
Stanley, G. S. 29, 30
Stansell, J. Harold 42
Staples, Dave 46
Steen, Ronald M. 198

T

Taylor, Cary A. 186
Thompson, A. H. 54
Thompson, Ty 152, 206, 212, 243
Thompson, Walter W. 40
Thorne, R. K. 29, 30, 31, 40
Thornton, Dave 170
Thornton, Larry D. 188, 260

U

Underwood, Lance 159
Underwood, Noah 11
Utley, W. Gary 191

V

Vandiver, N. A. 153

W

Wade, J. Cliff 220
Wagnon, Tim R. 158, 239
Walker, Eric L. 209
Walker, J. E. 122

Wallace, Curtis 187
Warhurst, Mike D.133,134, 157, 163, 226, 262
Watkins, Andrew 11
Weeks, Danny 170
Wells, Blaine W. 42, 55
Wells, Lon 37
Westbrook, J. E. 42
Westbrook, Walter 11
Williams, C. T. 11
Williams, Robert 165, 171
Willingham, Neal D. 241
Willis, Joe 201
Wilson, C. H. 37
Wilson, Floyd 37
Wilson, R. J. 13, 35
Wimbs, Sonny 255
Wimberly, Love 28
Winchester, Arthur C. 192
Wright, P. D. 132, 134, 157, 163, 226, 262
Wright, Waldo 29, 30

X

Y

Young, Carl F., Sr. 58
Young, Carl F., Jr. 188
Young, Harry, Jr. 38

Z

N O T E S

1 *TRAINS* magazine. September, 1997. pp 14-15.
2 Internet web site. Norfolk Southern electronic collection.
3 *TRAINS* magazine September, 1997. p 17 and p 89.
4. *Norfolk Southern Locomotive Directory 1998-1999*. p 119

BIBLIOGRAPHY

Magazines

Kevin P. Keefe. *Trains Magazine*. September, 1997.

Internet - Computer Electronic Data

Norfolk Southern Corporation. Corporate Communications.
NS@Norfolk.infi.net.

While every attempt has been made to secure permission from Norfolk Southern employees, Memphis & NA Districts, whose photographs appear in this book, we may have failed in a few cases to contact some employees. We apologize for any inadvertent oversight or error.